# OUTWITTING NEIGHBORS

# OUTWITTING

# NEIGHBORS

*Bill Adler, Jr.*

THE LYONS PRESS

Printed in Canada

Designed by Barbara M. Marks

10   9   8   7   6   5   4   3   2   1

The Library of Congress Cataloging-in-Publication Data
is available on file.

To:

*Anna*

*David*

*Dickson*

*Garry*

*Joan*

*John*

*Judy*

*Katherine*

*Leslie*

*Milton*

*Rives*

*Tom*

# ACKNOWLEDGMENTS

A book of this complexity is never a one-person task. Without the wonderful help of a number of people, *Outwitting the Neighbors* would still be just a good idea. I want to thank Peggy Robin, Elaine Viets, Beth Pratt-Dewey, Karin McDonald, Kara Leverte, Nick Viorst, Jane Dystel, and that guy in the apartment above me when I lived on 104th and Amsterdam in New York City.

# CONTENTS

# Introduction

*How I would love to spike their lawn with
poison ivy! and drop some sugar in their gas
tanks, especially the car they warm up thirty
minutes every morning just outside my
bedroom window; do mortal damage to the
lights they shine in my bedroom windows
all night, every night; glaze their
driveway with the beer bottles and trash
they throw on my side of the fence.*

—A NEIGHBOR

*Your next-door neighbor is not a man;
he is an environment. He is the barking
of a dog; he is the noise of a pianola; he
is a dispute about a party wall; he is
drains that are worse than yours,
or roses that are better than yours.*

—G. K. CHESTERTON, OVER
SEVENTY YEARS AGO

In the beginning there was this book proposal: *Outwitting the Neighbors*. And the proposal was submitted to several publishers, one of
whom, Fireside, accepted it and paid money; and lo, that was good.

Then there was an editor, Kara Leverte, at Fireside. And with
her worked an editorial assistant, Nick Viorst; and lo, there was the
problem.

You see, *Outwitting the Neighbors* was supposed to be a secret
from my neighbors. Right? Makes sense to me, anyhow. Keeping the
book a secret was particularly important because there are only
seven houses on our street in Washington, D.C., so we all know a lot
about our neighbors. Maintaining cordiality is important to the well-
being of all of us.

So, who is Nick Viorst? Nick is the son of the other Viorsts, whose house I can see very plainly from the room I'm currently writing this book in. And, I presume, the Viorsts can see my window clearly, too.

Well, so much for a secret book about neighbor problems. As Nick put it, *Outwitting the Neighbors* is about outwitting the Viorsts. Let me put it this way: When they saw a light burning late in the third-floor window of my house, they knew exactly what I was doing.

As it turns out, I have only good things to say—and think—about the people on my street, but this does prove that you have to be very careful about what you say about your neighbors.

Every American has neighbor problems. Neighbor wars affect the famous (you'll find some of those stories in these pages) as well as regular folk. If not today, then yesterday, and almost certainly tomorrow. One Phoenix, Arizona, judge estimates that some 45 percent of her cases are neighbor disputes. Some of these problems are benign annoyances. Some are silly. In one conflict one neighbor regularly threw apples at his neighbor's house, while the other neighbor mowed the lawn at 1 A.M. Some conflicts are apocalyptic. How bad can it get? Is there a hell, and if so, are there some neighbors who have just stopped by to your neighborhood on their way there? That's what Geoff Talcott must have thought about his downstairs neighbor, who on one occasion broke into his car, on another verbally harassed Talcott, and on yet another chased his twelve-year-old down the street. Talcott's neighbor even once tried to vent gas from his stove into Talcott's apartment. New Yorkers get it bad sometimes, but this was too bad, even for someone accustomed to New York City's griminess. (Fortunately for Talcott and his family, the neighbor now has new neighbors himself—other residents of a state mental hospital.)

Several years ago, a national survey was taken about neighbors. The results were surprising and disappointing. Two out of three Americans would rather discuss an important personal issue with a co-worker than with a neighbor.

Many events are altering our sense of community. Intense urbanization, large-scale development of neighborhoods, and changes in methods of transportation and communication are some of the factors that contribute to the loss of community that strikes many neighborhoods. Sending children to day care instead of having them around the house also contributes to deneighborhoodization. But a slow reversal of this trend may be taking place. More and more people are working at home, and this creates the opportunity for neighbors to get to know each other better.

• • • • • • • • • • • • • • • • • • • • • • • • • • • • • • • • • • • • • • • • • • • • • • • • • • • • • • • • •

> If you're thinking of renovating, build a front porch. Front porches go a long way toward encouraging neighborliness. The more often you wave "hi" to your neighbors, the better you get along with them.

• • • • • • • • • • • • • • • • • • • • • • • • • • • • • • • • • • • • • • • • • • • • • • • • • • • • • • • • •

Although it would have resulted in a slightly less comprehensive book, I could have relied exclusively on neighbor stories from my own neighborhood. But that, of course, would have created some, shall we say, problems, with my neighbors. So I've chosen not to write about what goes on in my Cleveland Park neighborhood—with two exceptions.

The first happened a few years before my wife and I moved into our house, so we can't claim any responsibility. Apparently, the owner of our house-to-be one day climbed to the roof and started firing a 22-caliber rifle. I didn't particularly mind moving into a house with such a history, and I can say for a fact that the other residents on the block were tickled to death (excuse the irresistible pun) that we were not NRA members.

The second story happened while I was researching this book. One windy wintry day, a storm passed through Washington, D.C. It was a malevolent storm, and it decided to hang out in Cleveland Park just long enough to let us know how strong and willful it was. At about 10 A.M. there was loud crack, followed immediately by an electric power outage. A hundred-year-old silver maple had just crossed the street and downed some power lines. That's often not so bad, but our heating system is powered by electricity and so is the videotape player that our two-and-a-half-year-old requires during the day. But I digress.

The downed tree was just half a block from our house, so I donned my ugliest coat and went out for a look. When power lines are crawling along the ground emergency services respond quickly. In minutes the fire department and power company were on the scene, trying to put things back as they had been.

As I was standing watching the tree that wasn't moving, a woman in her fifties approached me. "Excuse me," she said, "I live in that house and want to know when the power will be restored."

"Oh," I said, "I live in that house over there and I have no idea."

"Oh," she said. "I thought you worked for the power company." Does anybody know their neighbors?

Neighbor conflicts quickly and easily get out of control. Using neighbors as an example, it's easy to see how and why violent wars between nations start. Small disputes have the potential to erupt into uncontrollable conflict. And they will, unless some mediating force prevents this from occurring. Often, nations avoid war because their leaders are keenly aware of the death that accompanies war. They know the financial costs. They know about the damage to property. The leaders of nations know that often the head of state of the losing side loses his head—and somebody's got to lose.

But ordinary citizens have no such experience or knowledge. They don't know the consequences of neighbor wars. They don't know how annoyance turns into hatred; that neighbor wars divide communities; that these conflicts expose them to ridicule and worse; that if lawyers are involved their savings may be depleted. They don't know the amount of mental anguish involved. They don't know what harm may befall them for complaining. (Minneapolis estimates that 20 percent of criminal cases prosecuted by the city attorney's office begin with complaints from neighbors.)

Whenever possible, I've let the stories give advice, rather than giving it myself. You can learn a great deal from the successes or errors of others.

Remember, as you read these tales of woe: *there is another side to the story, which you may not be hearing.* Just because somebody has what sounds like a reasonable complaint against what appears to be an irrational neighbor, who's reasonable and who's not may not be as obvious as it seems. Neighbors at war have a way of shaping fact into fiction to suit their needs.

Rather than sanitize these quotations, I've left people's remarks about their neighbors as they are. Sometimes the opinions we hold of our neighbors are frightening; sometimes they are merely rude. But what's in *Outwitting the Neighbors* is, above all, what we really think. From the mouths of Americans, it's the truth.

There's a lot of good advice in this book—enough to save your sanity, enough to make you want to consider buying remote property in the Adirondacks or the Sierras, where you would have no near neighbors. A lot of the advice is common sense, a lot comes from conniving, well-planned strategies.

• • • • • • • • • • • • • • • • • • • • • • • • • • • • • • • • • • • • • • • • • • • • • • • • • • • • • • • •

## Neighbors and the Summer

Neighbor problems are worse in the summer than any other season. That's because we're outside more, our windows are open, and we see our neighbors more. If your neighbor bothers you in the summer, wait a season. See if time and the environment don't take care of the problem.

• • • • • • • • • • • • • • • • • • • • • • • • • • • • • • • • • • • • • • • • • • • • • • • • • • • • • • • •

While researching this book I spoke with people around the country. Without exception, everyone had a neighbor story to tell. If I could make *Outwitting the Neighbors* a large enough book, I suspect I could fill it with nearly 250 million stories.

One of my favorite bits of general advice came from a woman in the Midwest:

*Get along with your neighbors at all costs. Find out what they are like, and be flexible. It's the only solution, especially if you have children. They have to live there, too. It's too confusing if the parents are feuding and they are busy learning by example. They may someday need a friend, not an enemy.*

*If you can ignore the problem with your neighbor, do so. The problem will eventually disappear—teenagers eventually grow up; dogs die. I have found that when there are bad kids, speaking with the parents rarely works. For a speeding teenage driver, I erected my own barriers (picnic benches with SLOW signs). For kids who trample my bushes, a little manure helps, and for the barking dog, earplugs do the trick. What can you win, except stress, anger, and frustration? Not to mention the enemy nearby. Nothing. Just get along. Be cool. Calm down. The problem will eventually disappear. Life's too short. Keep*

•

*your sense of humor. Your kids will learn an invaluable lesson: Patience. Tolerance. Perseverance. Drive them crazy with your even temper. That's the best strategy.*

Throughout this book you'll find seemingly contradictory advice. In one paragraph compromise will be suggested; in the next the action will be more aggressive. These suggestions don't actually contradict each other—compromise and peaceful reconciliation with your neighbor is the best approach. But if there's a war, then you should try to be on the winning side.

# 1

# Cars and Parking

The two things Americans love most are their homes and their cars. Problems involving both may be the worst of all neighbor problems.

Of course, cars aren't really the trouble. It's their thoughtless owners. They exercise the engine at two in the morning before they go off to their night-shift jobs. They let rusting hulks rot in their yards and become havens for vermin. They drive on your lawn because they don't know how to back down their drives properly. They park in your reserved parking spot, or worse, they park on the street in front of your house—the place where you always park.

People take their parking spaces seriously. One New Yorker, who obviously didn't own the space on the street in front of him, put a note on any car that parked in front of his townhouse: "Park here again, and your car will be trashed." Nasty, but it did the trick.

One family had a feud over a parking space with another family, each claiming rights to the space. One side tried to block the other's car with logs; the other neighbor threatened to kill their cat and nail it to their door.

## PROTECTING YOUR CURB

Even as you read this, all over North America, people are driving up in front of their homes and parking. They don't even have to parallel park; they just pull up, grab their groceries, and run into the house. But others are circling the block again and again, cursing while the ice cream melts, the kids shriek, or the rain pelts. Someone is in "their" spot. When someone parks in their space, there's hell to pay.

Face it, people regard the curb in front of their home as their own.

June Geer, from Middletown, Ohio, says, "My ninety-year-old mother, who doesn't even own a car, let alone drive anymore, gets peeved when people park in front of her house. She tells her neighbors not to park there, and they don't." Maybe they respect age in Ohio; maybe the neighbors are especially understanding. Not everyone is as cooperative.

Consider this story from Curtis in St. Louis, Missouri.

*As you know, South St. Louis residents are very uptight about their parking places in front of their house. And the new kids on the block should respect that and use what space is left, right?*

*Well, this new kid across the street moved in with a pickup, three cars, a sailboat, and an overnight girlfriend with her own transportation. Soon the old-timers in the neighborhood began to see their parking spaces dwindling to a precious few. Complaints to the cops once in a while got the damn-near-thirty-foot-trailer-mounted sailboat off the street. That definitely was a no-no. But the various other vehicles were scattered about with abandon. And soon it became apparent that the parking spot in front of 1434 Northbrow was not the sacred ground it once had been.*

*Now, my housemate and I had only one car and needed only one spot, and since we decided we had seniority rights and possibly even squatters' rights, I took it upon myself to ask the new guy to park on his side of the street. That was not the best decision, since he in-*

*formed me he could damn well park anywhere he wanted. Okay, so whenever he occupied our spot, we parked in front of his house. That wasn't a wise decision either—he began parking one of his vehicles in front of our house and then when he was ready to move it he would get another one or have his girlfriend pull into our spot. So much for who won the first round.*

*I think we put up with this for three or four weeks and finally I got tired of the little fun and games and told him to stay out of the space or else. The "or else" being, I had all his license plates checked for authenticity, two showed up improper, and tickets were issued. Round two for me.*

*However, this didn't solve the problem; the tickets made our friendly neighbor unfriendly. So, soon, cars were again moving in and out of our parking spot like traffic on the city hall lot. Threats and words were exchanged again for a few more weeks, and of course the neighbors were getting prime-time entertainment from all the activity. When I overheard, "Gee, I wonder how long Curtis will put up with that?" that clinched it. I had to live up to my reputation.*

*I had to find my way to my tool room in the basement to get into full battle gear. I found my LIG sixteen-pounder and some goggles. That should do it. After all, I still had sense enough to realize that if I was going to smash something, I'd better protect my eyes from flying glass. I walked out to the front, sledgehammer in hand, goggles in place, and proceeded to knock out all the glass on vehicle one. That brought out neighbors I hadn't seen in months who egged me on to new efforts. So, fortified with attention, I proceeded across the street and finished off the pickup and two other cars. By that time the whole block was out and so were the cops (didn't know they could respond in a matter of minutes).*

*Well, they responded fast, but they were a little slow in taming me, and I hadn't finished yet. I would have been finished, since I had removed all the glass from all my neighbor's vehicles, but his girlfriend came out and shouted some uncouth remarks to me. I felt a little sorry for her, because, after all, she really didn't live in the neighborhood and didn't understand south St. Louis neighborhoods' unwritten law. If only she had not said anything. Well, I do remember my parents telling me to respect women, so I only hammered out her windshield and back window. And, at that, I was cuffed and stuffed.*

*As I said, "War is hell." And expensive too. Peace disturbance is somewhat costly, destruction of property is also costly, but "winning at*

•

*all costs" is the name of the game. I will conclude by saying I did win the war. Nobody for miles around parks in front of 1434 Northbrow to this day except the owner of the house.*

Sledgehammer to an offending vehicle.

Does this all-out nuclear annihilation of the problem seem, well, attractive in a perverse way? So what if you're arrested? That's a small price to pay for preserving your parking. We've all felt like torching (or using whatever tools happen to be around) a car that's parked in our space. But doing this is a sure path to Neighbor War, with inevitable escalation. That's what happened in one Phoenix, Arizona, neighborhood, where at least once every two weeks neighbors called the police on each other; or if the police were involved elsewhere, the zoning inspector, mostly over parking problems. When these neighbors had some spare time, they got court orders to thwart other neighbors' activities. Why? As one neighbor put it, "I decided what is good for the goose is good for the gander. I am not a person who is going to move someplace and allow other people to tell me how to live."

Act crazy or extreme, and your neighbors and friends will think you are crazy—with good reason.

What you have to do—absolutely have to—is pause before acting. Follow the advice of hundreds of $8.95 self-help books: take three deep breaths before doing anything. Plot and ponder, rather than taking immediate, swift, and irrevocable action. There are plenty of alternatives to damaging somebody's property. Does your neighbor block your driveway with his car? Then perhaps you should block his driveway (instead of letting the air out of his tires).

While you might give Curtis credit for trying to do things the right way (he first tried to reason with his neighbor), his attitude seems out of kilter. He started out on the wrong foot when he told his neighbor he had "seniority rights and possibly even squatters' rights."

Things could have happened differently. Let's chart out a different course of action for the same situation:

- Curtis takes initial dislike to neighbor (because he has too many material possessions.)
- He chats him up despite his dislike.
- The neighbor invites him to go sailing.

- They share adventure and a few beers.
- The neighbor still parks the boat in front of Curtis's house but tells him to use it whenever he likes.

Not a bad resolution. Or maybe the neighbor takes care of Curtis's cat when he's out of town.

Of course you realize you don't own the street in front of your house, and you can't (that's shouldn't) prevent people from parking there. But most people are reasonable and will make concessions, like parking elsewhere, in view of the combat injury that prevents you from walking long distances. (*Of course* you're making this up.)

Take the neighbor who parked his car so that it blocked the sidewalk. This neighbor eventually stopped when another neighbor told him how difficult it was for her to stroll her baby carriage by.

If a little friendly reasoning doesn't work, you might try making it unpleasant for your neighbors to continue parking in your spot. Place smelly garbage on the curb. Put a bird feeder in the trees overhanging the street so that the bird mess falls directly on your neighbor's car. (That technique works especially well for new cars.) Keep a fierce dog in the front yard. Put cat food on the car so that cats during the day and raccoons at night leave little paw prints on the car. Plant a curbside garden and fertilize it heavily with manure. But remember: construction debris (nails) innocently spilled into the parking space is too much.

While these techniques may seem a bit nasty, they're certainly less offensive than damaging somebody's car. I'm not recommending them and have never tried them myself, but if it's a war you have, well then, winning is better than losing. Do what you have to, some people say.

Alternatively, you can learn your neighbor's schedule and make sure your car is always in place when the neighbor is looking for parking. Eventually he'll start parking elsewhere.

Finally, consider building a carport and park in your front yard. Alison Fox tried a variation on this solution, but her neighbors objected. The seventy-year-old Mokena, Illinois, resident started parking on the grass in her front yard when nerve damage from two back surgeries made negotiating the seven steps from her drive to her door unmanageable. Unfortunately parking in your front yard is illegal in Mokena, and her neighbors complained to the officials. They wanted her to install either a ramp or a circular drive and offered to help pay for the construction. Fox stiffened her spine, rejected their offers, and placed her home on the market, although moving is an extreme solution and one that few can afford when they have parking problems.

As in any neighbor-neighbor disagreement, bringing officialdom into the mix causes relations to deteriorate and makes it difficult to reach any sort of amicable solution. Before the authorities were called in, perhaps Fox and her neighbors could have worked out their problems with a mediator, but afterward, there were probably too many bad feelings to reach any sort of useful solution.

Just be glad you're not up against Luke Saunders from Painesville Township in Ohio, just outside Cleveland. He's the owner of a neighborhood diner that is quickly running out of room for customer parking. The township's trustees won't change the zoning to allow him to offer parking across the street in a lot he owns. Neighbors object, because they don't want to live among a sea of parked vehicles. Despite the opposition, Saunders is offering a reward of $50,000 to anyone who can persuade the township's trustees to allow him to use his empty lot for parking. His unusual tactics landed him a story in the *National Enquirer*, and "This Week with David Brinkley" even taped a show on site. The neighbors won in this case, and Saunders has to make do with the parking he has.

Still, the tactic has some merit. If all else fails, pay someone not to park in front of your house.

..........................................................

## CURBSIDE COURTESY. TACTICS TO PROTECT YOUR TURF

Change your work hours so you and your neighbor use the space at different times.

Park an RV in front of the house and don't move it (at least your neighbor can't use the spot).

Move to the country and park in front of your door.

..........................................................

## RENTER PARKERS

People who rent houses can be particularly troublesome when it comes to parking. Renters are often not acquainted with the customs that year-round neighbors abide by.

In one ski resort town, the locals on a particular road all chipped in for snow removal, which can be expensive, as upward of six hundred feet have to be plowed several times a year. The renters on the road weren't inclined to contribute and made their opinions known to the resident who did the money collecting by "spending time in my driveway at about three A.M. screaming obscenities at me and throwing beer cans at my house." The money-collecting neighbor added, "By springtime when the snowpack melts they then vent their emotions by driving their four-wheelers on my lawn."

What can you do about unruly renters? For starters, make sure that they aren't invited back the following year by the homeowner who rented the house. Or you can bide your time, as this homeowner did. "I can be provoked, but to date I have held my temper and remained out of jail. It can't last forever, though." The renters will soon be gone.

Or, while the renters are around, lay down the law. If they won't cooperate, use your association's, community's, or city's clout to make them cooperate. That's what one homeowners association member did when some renters used their parking space as a makeshift auto-repair shop:

*Five single guys, sharing a rental house, bought an incredibly beat-up Dodge 4WD pickup and began working on it. They wanted to change out the front axle and their driveway wasn't level enough, so they parked it sticking out into the cul-de-sac turnaround, blocked up the front end, and dropped the axle. No big deal.*

*Two weeks later, it began to get old. Six weeks later, people were getting pissed. Finally someone, I don't know who, complained to the city. A deputy showed up with a tow truck and hauled it off.*

## PARKING SPACE THIEVERY

Sometimes the parking space in front of your house really is your own: a parcel about the size of those offered for sale in Arizona through comic books. Many condos, townhouses, or apartments have assigned parking. That means you always have your spot reserved for your exclusive use. Right? Well, not always. There are always people who don't even notice the eye-catching reserved signs and colorful numbers painted on the asphalt. Perhaps they're visitors from another planet and don't understand the cultural significance of a reserved parking space. But perhaps they're your neighbors, and they violate your parking space again and again. What should you do then?

In Alexandria, Virginia, one neighbor had a third party mediate his parking problem—a towing company.

When Betsy Mantz and two roommates were moving into their new condo, they simply pulled up their moving van and started unloading. Since not everything fit into the van, one of the roommate's cars was stuffed full of belongings. Unfortunately, it was parked in their neighbor's reserved parking spot. His weapon of choice? Not face-to-face confrontation but the tow truck. Before they knew it, the packed car was hooked onto a tow truck. Fifty dollars later, the car was retrieved and parked elsewhere, and the next morning a the condo official rules were on the doorstep with the paper.

Having your new neighbor's car towed isn't the best way to start a neighborly relationship. Like many impetuous and quick solutions, it creates more problems of its own. When you need to borrow a ladder, to whom will you go? Who will help you move a heavy piece of furniture? Certainly not the neighbor whose car you had towed.

If life didn't already have too many rules, I'd suggest the following: On moving day, people can park in any empty spot they find—as long as they don't block other people. But they should ask first. Alternatively, advance warning works: Just tell your neighbor that you're moving in and you might need to borrow his parking space. Your neighbor will be so shocked that you asked, that he or she will almost certainly say yes. He'll be bewildered by your thoughtfulness, too.

Sometimes you catch people in the act of stealing your space, as John McVicar,* the British journalist and former bank robber, did.

*A neighbor tried to nick my parking place. So I blocked her off. She nipped out of her car, ran over, and let my tires down. So I let hers down. Suddenly I could see it creeping into eternity like that. You find yourself acting like a little kid, getting very neurotic about it all. The*

*Real name

*trouble with tit for tat is that you might get the tat on the very day you're running late for something important.*

But what about the habitual parking-space abuser? Say your neighbor owns a particularly bad parking spot, one under the exhaust fan in the parking garage or next to the Dumpster outside, and parks in your space all the time. Attempt the official method, which is what worked for a man outside Philadelphia: Try blocking your space with some orange traffic cones. People are rarely bold enough to actually remove them. They'll skulk into someone else's space— or maybe even their own! As soon as the thief is trained, remove the cones.

Fighting fire with fire sometimes works. A woman named Laurie relates this story:

*A friend of mine had a parking-space dispute with one of her neighbors a while back. The condo complex she lived in was configured in square clusters. Since her unit was the longest walk from the parking lot, she was assigned the space most convenient to the walkway to her unit. One of her neighbors, whose own space was being used by his girlfriend, began parking every evening in her space even though it had her unit number painted on the curb. Mind you, there was plenty of unassigned parking around the complex, but the spaces weren't as convenient as hers.*

*She tried to talk to him about it and complained to the homeowners association, but it didn't do any good. Finally, one morning, she spied his assigned space empty, made a deal with her car pool to trade a week's driving, and parked her car in his space for more than a week. Needless to say, the guy wasn't happy about it at all, but he finally got the message and stopped parking in her space.*

Because a parking-spot thief is a criminal of sorts (in your eyes), he's going to be defensive if you have to confront him verbally. Unlike someone who isn't aware that his pogo-sticking at 2 A.M. is bothersome, a parking-space thief probably knows that he is a rotten scoundrel. Parking-space thieves wear guilt the way you and I wear socks. Still, it's worth trying to approach the parking thief to get some relief. Act as if you think he isn't even aware of assigned parking. "Hey, did you know those numbers painted in each parking space actually correspond to our apartment numbers?" Some people are willing to be anonymous jerks but not public ones, so a simple word will do. If the response is "Oh, sorry," then those dozen or so words have just made your life better in a big way. If the response is "So what?" you've got a problem. Maybe it's time for the tow truck or a complaint to the homeowners association.

Towing is a hostile act and one of last resort. It's ridiculous to feign ignorance of your neighbor's make of car when you've had it towed away. You recognize your neighbors' cars the way you recognize your own shoes. You and he both know who did what to whom. Always warn (or attempt to warn) and then act. Many housing associations employ a private towing company to haul off scofflaws. Cities are usually amiable about towing a working car because they can be pretty sure someone will claim it.

If your neighbor has parked a junked car in your space, you have a rougher assignment. Nobody likes towing an undrivable car, because there's no place to put it. In this case, consult your city's ordinances about getting a car declared abandoned. (More on this later.)

Theatrical acts like calling in tow trucks are a deterrent at condos and apartments, too. Most people live where gossip is the predominant means of communication, so the person you really want to reach will get the message. Towing frightens people.

When there isn't any reserved parking, you take what you can get. But that doesn't mean anarchy. Rules still apply, and you set the tone for parking civility by obeying them. Because many parking lots are isolated, it's not always a good idea to pick a fight over a parking spot. It may earn you a quick trip to the hospital—or worse.

If the unwritten rule on your street is "Don't park in front of a neighbor's house for more than a few minutes," then don't. That's the rule where I live. Now there's nothing the residents of my street can do about people who park for the nearby movie theater. (Nearby is one-third of a mile, but when parking is tight, distance is relative.) Everybody on my block knows that we just don't park in front of a neighbor's house. If a moviegoer's car is in front of your house, well, then you have to park somewhere else, no matter how far that somewhere else is. This is how we preserve parking civility where I live. It works.

But I happen to be lucky. Witness what others go through. In Round Lake Beach, Illinois, a man was jailed after threatening to strike a neighbor, a woman, during a dispute over a parking space. And in West Mifflin, Pennsylvania, a man stabbed and killed a neighbor during a dispute over a parking space. In Santa Clara, California, a man shot and killed his neighbor during a long-simmering feud over parking, overgrown vegetation, and pets.

Sure, these stories seem extreme. Until they become your own. I saw a mother have her twelve-year-old son let the air out of the tires of a car that was parked in her space. Stay away from verbal sparring over parking spaces and save your energies for plotting devious ways to make a parking spot your own.

........................................................................

## PARKING LOT WAR RULES

For maximum impact and parking-spot protection, the towing of a vehicle in violation must be witnessed by the maximum number of neighbors.

You can't tow emergency vehicles from your parking lot.

Disagreeing with the political message on your neighbor's bumper sticker is not a reason to tow.

........................................................................

# UNSIGHTLY HULKS, USED CAR LOTS, AND RV STORAGE

Some people are just unable to part with a car, no matter that it hasn't run for years. And they're in every neighborhood, urban or rural, tony or grungy. Some hulks have innocent beginnings as a car that just won't start. But instead of fixing them or towing them, the owners just hang on, too sentimental or too cheap or too busy to do anything. Other people collect cars the way some hobbyists collect stamps.

These cars or trucks become a major source of bad feeling among neighbors. They're ugly (well, most people think so), they just about kill the sales potential of your house, and cats die from drinking the leaking antifreeze. They become havens for every sort of rodent except bunnies. Even though abandoning vehicles in the street or even storing broken-down jalopies on your property is illegal in most jurisdictions, people flout the law. Many municipalities don't enforce abandoned-car rules unless there's a complaint. Al-

·

though police or cities have the right to order the removal of the vehicles or even have them towed, they're often slow to act or busy elsewhere—probably because they're stopping fistfights between neighbors on the block or busy dealing with one particular Chicago, Illinois, woman.

This woman claimed her hulk wasn't an abandoned or disabled vehicle. It was art. In her well-to-do suburb of Chicago, the junker car was part of a front-yard display titled "The Monument to Humanity No One Will Be Able to Build After George Bush Has His Winnable Limited Protracted Nuclear War With 20 Million Americans Acceptable Loss." Artist Ruth Ruckert attracted national attention when she went to court to protect her display, which included a station wagon, tree stumps, kitchen cabinets, and forty-two tons of sand. She lost but had a sense of humor and fairness about the situation and toted the trash off to another location, where she plans to reassemble it.

Why is it so hard to get junker cars off the streets (or out of your neighbor's driveway)? In Orange County, California, alone, there are nearly 46,000 complaints a year over cars abandoned on public and private property. And only about a fifth of those cars are towed. Are the remaining 37,000 hulks rehabilitated into moving vehicles or artwork? They're probably still there annoying the neighbors.

Cities are hesitant to tow hulks because it's expensive, and it's not as if the junkers bring in a lot of municipal cash, even if they are auctioned off. Frequently, it can be difficult to try to haul off someone's treasured junk. They fight, most often in court. Neighbors aren't just lazy or too cheap to dispose of their junked cars; they actually want them.

It's an old saw, but it bears repeating here: one man's junk is another man's treasure. An Orange County resident, Mark Zamry, kept half a dozen vintage Cadillacs on his property. His pride and joy. His neighbors found his collection so unsightly that they petitioned to have the cars removed. Zamry fought them every step of the way and won a small victory when the judge allowed him to keep one of his Cadillacs, which Zamry managed to start when the judge visited. The other five are gone.

Going at a problem singlehandedly is a tiresome, lonely task. There's a much better strategy: When all the neighbors gang up on a problem, it gets solved. That's what happened in Burbank, California.

After neighbors filed a complaint, officials towed off two cars, a van, and a pickup truck from Bea and Ron Young's drive. Officials declared the vehicles junk and then hauled them away three days after the Youngs were given their final warning to rehabilitate or move the vehicles. Because they had ignored many earlier warnings, they lost their cars. It seemed reasonable to the neighbors (and to me, frankly) that five broken-down cars should be towed, but the Youngs fought the action. In this case, the system worked, but probably not as quickly as the neighbors wished.

So what can you do about rusting hulks? Some pretty creative action is called for. You can try offering to pay for the towing yourself. You can offer to garage the junker for the owner—at least until you sell your house. Think of ways to hide the car—a screening fence, a row of hedges, or moving it behind the house. Maybe just a canvas car cover will improve things. When you make suggestions to the neighbor, offer to help carry out the plan. That makes it more difficult to reject the offer.

If you suspect that the car is attracting rodents, call the health department. Health officials have considerable powers and often act more swiftly than the car police. Indeed, cars that attract rats and other rodents are a public health hazard.

Consider your alternatives very carefully, though. Sometimes complaining just makes you look like a lout. Jean Smith, like many other people across the country, had a recreational vehicle parked in her driveway. What was different in this situation was her cousin, near death from terminal ovarian cancer, lived in the RV despite a local ordinance that prohibited people from living in their vehicles. The neighbors complained, despite the bad press they received. But before the city could enforce the prohibition, the unfortunate woman died. After the funeral, friends hung a banner on the RV, reading "Farewell, Linda, Farewell." Surely the neighbors hung their heads in shame.

Often there's a "good reason" why a car is someplace it shouldn't be. One frosty January I received a hundred-dollar parking ticket because the registration sticker on my car had expired. I protested the ticket, not because it was unwarranted, but because I had the flu and didn't want to venture outside to play with my car's license plate in the middle of winter. The city reduced my fine by fifty dollars.

Not all cases are so dramatic. There's nothing wrong with simply not liking the looks of an RV cluttering up your neighborhood. There's no beauty in a boat on a trailer if you're not the person who gets to enjoy sailing every weekend. But unless some local ordinance forbids RV storage, you probably just have to get used to it, unless your neighbor is way out of control. Some hobbyists are so caught up in their interests that they lose all objectivity.

That happened in Largo, Florida, where B. J. Covington has had two airplanes parked in his front yard for nearly ten years. The inoperable planes were too large to fit in the backyard, and the city was after him to get a new home for them, but he wasn't doing anything illegal. Covington didn't want to move the planes, and so they stayed. If any of his neighbors are reading this book (I hope so!) here's an idea: take up a collection to have the planes repaired or stored at a local airfield.

Recreational vehicles are a tough problem, because most jurisdictions will allow them to be stored on private property, with some limits on size and location. (Large vehicles often must be screened from view or kept in certain places.) So, often you have no choice but to live with a camper in the backyard or drive. Sorry. But if you're nice about the issue, one day your neighbor will be happy to hide the RV during your daughter's wedding reception, held in your lovely garden.

Appearances aren't the worst problems of recreational vehicles either. A man who wishes to remain anonymous had to tolerate his neighbor, an avid boater and fisherman, who stored his boat in his backyard all year. But there was worse: whenever the fisherman cleaned his catch, he tossed the fish and crab entrails into his neighbor's yard.

## WHEN NEIGHBORS BECOME USED CAR MERCHANTS

It's no crime to be an entrepreneur, right? You wouldn't begrudge your neighbor a little extra cash, would you? Well, yes and no. Sometimes your neighbor's business can get downright pesky.

Allen and Anna Gordon, struggling to keep up with their mortgage payments, tried a number of strategies to stay afloat after Allen was laid off from his job as heavy-equipment diesel mechanic. They considered a number of options, but settled on something that took advantage of Allen's skills and the Gordons' resources.

The Gordons turned to repairing old cars for resale. In time, their yard became cluttered with broken-down vehicles and signs advertising the cat's stud service (as if the world needed more cats) and garage sales. Someone complained to city officials who fined the Gordons for violating vehicle and zoning codes by operating a used-car business without a license in a residential area. Rather than fighting to protect their right to create an eyesore, the couple put the home up for sale.

If you don't want to report your neighbor, maybe you can work out a compromise about hours of operation or the state of the work site. It's worth a try, and who knows, you might find a good, local mechanic who will work cheap!

•••••••••••••••••••••••••••••••••••••••••••••••••••••••••••••••••••

## About Being a Tattletale

Most cities let you tattle on your neighbor anonymously. But if your neighbor is persistent enough, he can find out who ratted. If you've been complaining to your neighbor regularly, he'll have a reasonably good guess. In some cases, city officials inadvertently reveal who complained.

And remember—unless you live a squeaky-clean life, your neighbor will always be able to find something to reveal about you.

•••••••••••••••••••••••••••••••••••••••••••••••••••••••••••••••••••

Still, if you get no cooperation from your neighbor, pick up the phone. Backyard repair shops are against the law in many places, and it's not surprising that home mechanics are often reported anonymously—by licensed repair shops. It should be easy to get the city to crack down. Most people halt as soon as they receive notice from the city. If your community doesn't have a ruling against illegal businesses, look for creative ways to get at the neighbor. He may be violating noise ordinances or pollution laws. (What does he do with all that oil?)

Let your conscience help you decide whether to report an illegal business to the city. As always, be careful when you tattle.

•

Car repair isn't just unsightly, it's often noisy. Sometimes you might imagine you're living above the Indianapolis Motor Speedway when your neighbor is revving his car engine at 5 A.M. But you don't have it as bad as residents of a Tarpon Springs, Florida, neighborhood. Resident Scott Austin raced his Chevy Vega, which runs on methanol, on weekends and tuned it up every week—gunning the engine for two minutes or more. Imagine an Indianapolis 500 repair pit beneath your window. His neighbors complained and they all ended up in the Citizens Settlement Dispute Program. Unfortunately they couldn't settle their differences there either. Austin refused to allow officials to measure the noise levels when he tuned his car, and the neighbors refused his compromise to limit the revving to certain hours. They just want him to stop entirely. And so they remain with everybody suffering.

These neighbors still have options. First, limiting noisemaking hours is a step forward. It means that all sides recognize that the noise is a problem. Wait a while, then limit the hours more. Every few months, or every year, continue to apply pressure by further curtailing work time.

Alternatively, the neighbors could take a completely different tack and go after the car for its threats to safety. Methanol is highly flammable and may be banned as a dangerous substance in residential areas. Sometimes a little technology can help in the courtroom. Neighbors could have measured the noise levels of the revving engine and checked to see if the sound exceeded levels set by local ordinance. (The government needs permission; individuals can just take a noise meter to the source.) They could audiotape or even videotape a tune-up session.

A videotape helped some suburban Houston neighbors win their battle against the car. Although he had been ordered in 1990 to cease parking his one-ton flatbed trucks at his home for extended periods, Max Bassil continued until he stacked up sixty violations. His neighbors, tired of the flatbed trucks in front of his house, videotaped his infractions and charged him with violating the homeowners association rules. At one time, Bassil parked a truck marked "oxidized cargo" at the house. (That translates into dangerous stuff.) In the end, he went to jail for ten days and paid a $5,500 fine.

．．．．．．．．．．．．．．．．．．．．．．．．．．．．．．．．．．．．．．．．．．．．．．．

## BEATING THE MECHANIC BLUES

Send your neighbor to accounting school to learn a new trade. (This isn't as farcical a notion as you might think. Think about it.)

Be creative. If the business regulation department won't get after the mechanic, try environmental regulation or public safety.

Work out a compromise. He changes your oil for free and you live with the mechanical mess next door.

．．．．．．．．．．．．．．．．．．．．．．．．．．．．．．．．．．．．．．．．．．．．．．．．．．．．．．．．．

# 2

# Condos, Coops, and Homeowners Associations

*Personally, I deliberately live in a subdivision that's a bit less than beautiful. Nobody has any pretensions of living in an upper-class neighborhood; the homeowners association, which is supposed to police the covenants, barely has the income to keep the lawn mowed in the park and certainly couldn't hire a lawyer; and we all cut one another some slack. Result: I can park my twenty-six-foot sailplane trailer, run a big antenna, fly my R/C model helicopter in the green-space—no problem. We get some loud music, dis-assembled cars in driveways . . . but we get along.*
—ONE NEIGHBOR'S SOLUTION
TO HOMEOWNERS ASSOCIATION PROBLEMS

While petty, pesky, and eccentric neighbors appear everywhere, they can really get under your skin when they have the power to tell you what to do. And that's pretty much the situation when you live in a condominium, coop, or subdivision governed by a homeowners association. Condo boards and homeowners associations are your peers, your neighbors, who volunteer to keep life running smoothly for everyone. In theory. In reality, they're often your annoying, nosy, smug neighbors. Sometimes they come to your rescue (when they can stop that annoying noise from next door), but they can also object to the new coat of paint on your front door. So you love them and you hate them. Associations can turn ordinary disputes into mega-conflicts. Why? Because there's politics involved.

Condos have been around a long time. They existed in sixth-century B.C. Rome (and were no doubt unearthed by archaeologists who found condo board members still in a meeting over assessments for a new roof). So by now residents should have figured out how to coexist. Right? Not necessarily.

One condo resident was so fed up with the noise in the apartment below, that he drilled holes in his floor and poured gasoline down.

Over the centuries, homeowner problems have spread. More and more communities are choosing rule by association. The first homeowners association popped up about twenty-five years ago, and now about 80 million Americans live in housing governed by community associations, groups formed to maintain community property. Much falls under their purview—fences, paint, decorations, and house additions—so much that you can hardly make a move without consulting them. You want a pet? Ask first. You want to hang Christmas lights? Submit your plan in writing. You want a new refrigerator? There's no delivery on Tuesdays or Thursdays.

It's easy to forget these associations serve a very important function: They manage the jointly held property of the group—lakes, roofs, parking garages, landscaped areas, and community rooms. And they enforce the rules, the ones you didn't bother to read when you moved in. And with about 150,000 different condo and homeowners associations, that's a lot of rules and regulations.

In the end, the rules grate on people. You expect autonomy in your home, no matter what agreements you signed, but one day a board member shows up to point out your new outside gas lamp violates community covenant 1,267, part A, section 43. The people grate on you, too. You're not used to communal living and compromise for the greater good. There are skirmishes over balcony barbecues. Battles over children skateboarding.

Finally there's all-out war. Over issues like noise. Over who washed fuzzy bathroom rugs and left the washers full of lint. Over trash. Decorations. Parties. Parking (of course). Pets. In homeowners associations, problems are rarely between individual neighbors; they almost always involve The Board.

Sometimes residents don't even know the rules until they receive a notice pointing out that the two-inch mezuzah, a Jewish emblem, on the front door is in violation of the association rules.

•

Sometimes the associations are strangely silent—like when you really need them to enforce the rules against your neighbor's fifteen-foot satellite dish.

Homeowners associations are comprised of people, and hence are illogical, emotional, arbitrary, and sometimes just plain vindictive. What do you do when your neighbors, in the guise of the association, gang up on you?

In almost all states, the only recourse for association members with a gripe is to let a court decide. Most disputes arise when an association member chafes at the rules. People don't read their agreements closely or they want a special exception for their Santa-with-eight-reindeer-crèche-snowman display but not for their neighbor's new purple shutters.

Courts tend to side with associations. More on this later.

## AT ONE WITH THE ASSOCIATION

Your neighbor's husband won't let her smoke in the apartment so she does it in the hallway. Before you know it, your apartment (not to mention the hallway) smells like an ashtray. Sound unlikely? Just the opposite—it happens often. Who will come to your aid? The husband? No, he's happy with the situation. The woman? What's she going to do? Take the elevator down seven stories to have a smoke? Homeowners association to the rescue!

For all the bad press associations get, they're often useful because they have the teeth to enforce the rules, rules you should read before you move in. When there's a neighbor who's violating your tranquillity—and the association's rules—that inflexible, pigheaded, rotten condo board can be your greatest ally. Some associations can levy fines, as well. They can ban offenders from using common property like gyms and pools. They can institute a lawsuit for you against an offending neighbor. They can fight the fights you're too busy to fight. They have the clout of a city government, because in some ways, they are a city government.

Many of the residents in association-ruled communities like the situation. They move into condos with homeowners associations because of the stability, predictability, quiet, and orderliness they offer. Plenty of people look for associations with particular rules: no pets, no loud music, no children. They're tired of looking at kids' bikes on the lawn, landscaping they consider unsightly, and old clunkers in the driveway. They *crave* rules and order—the exact height of hedges, the angle of handrails, and when leaves must be raked—and an association provides that.

Associations are also handy for organizing people to sue a shoddy developer when roofs are leaking or to fight a planned power plant.

There are plenty of success stories of homeowners associations successfully waging battle for residents against developers and other interlopers who seek to ruin the lives of people who live there, so there are plenty of occasions when members are relieved to belong to the association—especially when the problems involve millions of dollars. In Washington D.C., for example, residents of the infamous Watergate complex fought a city plan to house five hundred homeless people outside their door. After a protracted battle, they won.

Mad about the illegal air-conditioning units in the windows of the house next door? A job for the homeowners association. Your neighbor painted her house shocking pink? Call up your association board members. While Congress may deliberate for years and years before legislation is passed, associations can act within a couple of hours. And if an annoyance isn't on the books, call a special meeting to discuss the issue. Maybe your pet peeve can be against the rules too. Association rules aren't the Ten Commandments. They can change and adapt to new community needs.

In one case, in Somerset, Massachusetts, the homeowners association's new rules limit tree height and the size of house additions. Anticipating a crisis, this association board had had the foresight to modify their rules on these issues before things heated up. Recognizing that many of their community members would want to remodel their twenty-five-year-old homes, they set up regulations to limit the size of additions so no one would lose a view. They also mandated a maximum tree size. When the original rules were adopted no one thought to include a size limitation, because the trees were just saplings. The board reactivated an architectural committee to review any building plans and they're also setting up a mediation board. Because many disagreements between neighbors ultimately end up in the courts, the association added that one last regulation. Now neighbors have to try to mediate before suing. In addition, the new rules reflect reality, the fact that people in the com-

•

munity own boats and trailers that they use. So the new rules allow them.

Rules can be changed. For the most part, association boards are begging for people to serve, so you can make a big difference if you have an agenda. I know, because I once serve on a condo board. In fact, apathy is the biggest problem for many boards. No one wants to manage the community, no one wants to attend meetings. Nobody wants to take the heat for problem after problem. Condos, coops, and homeowners associations never have enough money, but there are always projects that have to be completed. It's the quintessential thankless job. After all, everybody expects the elevator to be kept running, but nobody in the building likes a special assessment that the board has to levy to pay for those repairs.

If you have a pet peeve about the way your neighbors behave, the best way to change things is to run for the board—and win. Being on the board gives you the power to change your neighborhood for the better. Once on the board you'll have an opportunity to cajole other members to vote your way. Trading votes on condo boards is a common occurrence. Vote my way on fines for illegal pets, and I'll vote with you on painting the third floor green. All over America, every day, association boards are trading integrity for tranquillity.

Sometimes the association wins when face-to-face neighbor negotiations fail. Condo residents in Houston, Texas, learned that lesson when they couldn't get their neighbor to discover the volume knob on his stereo. They tried talking to him, writing diplomatic notes, and pounding on the walls. So they called their condo board president. The board had leverage and could fine the noisy neighbor for his loutish behavior. The blow to his checking account worked wonders and now the neighboring couple enjoys peace.

••••••••••••••••••••••••••••••••••••••••••••••••••••••••••••••••

## How to Make the Most Out of Your Board

Become active in politics: get a seat on your board.

Familiarity breeds helpfulness. Become familiar with your board members even if you don't want to serve. Make yourself attend at least one meeting that's not the annual one. Then, when you complain, board members will remember you showed an interest in the community and be more quick to help you than someone they've never met.

Read your rules before you buy, not when you get a notice of a violation.

Get to know your neighbors. Creating a voting block when it comes to election time can help. There may actually be some board members who covet reelection.

If you're thinking of investing in real estate, buy more property in your association (assuming the bylaws allow you to rent). This will give you more voting shares, and make you a more powerful association member. By investing where you live, you'll have more control over your own destiny.

## At War with the Association

Your association's rule against basketball hoops seemed perfectly reasonable—until your son reached puberty and developed a keen interest in rimshots. So you put a net up over your garage, and your son practiced setups with his pals after school and on Saturday afternoons. Then one day you get a notice in your mailbox reminding you that your backstop is an illegal structure. What do you do? Fight or flight?

It's not an easy decision. Any fight with a homeowners association means a fight with your neighbors. When tempers flare in the meeting room, you still have to deal with the same people in the laundry room. Is it worth the fight? You have to decide beforehand how much you'll fight and how far you'll take the battle.

Things seem to escalate to ridiculous levels in individual versus association fights, probably because people can focus all their frustrations about their homes on a single person or group of people. Some people spend thousands of dollars fighting cases, and the only thing they get is two inches of coverage in the *National Enquirer* and a hefty legal bill. And when people fight homeowners associations in court, they pay double. Their dues and fees pay in part for the association's legal fees as well as their own legal fees.

Before you fight, take an informal poll of your neighbors. If most of your immediate neighbors aren't bothered by your yodeling practice at 9 P.M. you may be able to convince the board that there's no problem. Your neighbors may support you on any number of issues—where boats are stored, the range of paint colors allowed for homes, or the types of lighting fixtures permitted. Try getting your supporters to join you at a board meeting; you may be able to get what you want if you show enough people are on your side. One time-honored way to gather support is to offer to trade support for you in return for your supporting something that your neighbors want. (Alternatively—remember, this book is also about winning the war—you can mention that you won't mention their illegal cat or subtenant, if they stand behind you.)

Not everyone has the "us versus them" mentality. Sometimes the neighbors side with the association—especially when the issue affects their pocketbook. If you lash out against the association, you may harm your neighbors. People who previously have not taken sides over your fight with the association may now line up against you.

That's what Dave Ger found out when he posted bright orange signs around his home near San Diego. The signs announced that his $160,000 townhouse was contaminated by mold and a jury had found the homeowners association liable for the damage. Frustrated by the association's slowness to pay up, Ger posted the signs.

His neighbors, some of whom were struggling to sell their own homes, fought back. He had taken their community fight public. In retaliation, Ger found his home splattered with eggs.

This battle started when Ger's eldest son developed respiratory problems soon after the family moved into the house; his allergies were traced to molds in the home. Ger thought the association was at fault because it failed to repair a roof leak. The courts agreed and ordered the association to pay $108,000 in damages, mostly for medical costs. Ger also fell behind in his mortgage payments because he had to move his family into a rental home.

Then both sides appealed; the homeowners association because they didn't want to pay, and Ger because he wanted more money. When the two sides couldn't come to an agreement about the money, Ger posted the signs. His neighbors turned against him, charging that he had exaggerated his troubles to solve his financial problems.

As Ger learned too late, it's useful to have your neighbors on your side. When your neighbors side with you, you seem more reasonable, more deserving of what you seek and it makes the board seem like some meddlesome group of busybodies.

When you can't get any response from your condo board,

what's the next step? Some folks opt for the dramatic.

Condo associations can take action first and ask questions later. This is what happened to Ben Blanchard, a California resident. When Blanchard discovered that his house was built on an oil waste dump, he sued the condo association and everyone else involved. After waiting four years for the suit to come to a conclusion, he decided to take matters into his own hands and he erected a sign on top of his house announcing that the house was built on top of a waste depot. The association had some people scale his roof and tear the sign down. Blanchard put it back up and sued again. As I write this book, the case is still in court.

You may find it's easier to fight the rules from the inside out. Try to run for a seat on your community's association and change the rules then. You don't have to serve forever; a year is enough. Being a past secretary or president affords you some amount of status in the community. People will respect your opinion and turn to you for advice. Best of all, when you speak at a board meeting, people will listen.

Be warned though. The job is a tough one. It's amazing that anyone volunteers to serve at all. A 1987 survey of condominium and homeowners associations for the state of California found that 44 percent of board presidents reported board members had been harassed or subjected to personal abuse or threatened with a lawsuit.

Before you start your battle, decide how far you'll go. All too often, solving the problems shrinks in importance and fighting the association's board becomes all-consuming. In Fairfax, Virginia, a clash over costs of repairing balconies escalated into emotional meetings that inspired one board member to hide a tape recorder. When the recorder was discovered, the other residents brought video equipment to record the next board meeting. Soon everyone was in a court of law when the board wanted to destroy their audiotapes and stop the videotaping.

Before you fight, find out if you have a case and if you have any support. Think about what you'll do if you lose. Will you spend five hundred dollars to fight the ruling? How about five thousand dollars? Will you give up your weekends for legal research? Sometimes it's easier to cut your losses and move. Remember, this is all about living—not fighting.

•  •  •

•

## A Tip on Losing

If you think you're going to lose or have lost on an important issue—say, having a pet or using your house to run a mail-order business—there's no need to give in immediately. Negotiate a time period within which you will either stop the offensive activity or leave. If you can convince the board that it make more sense for them to let you and your family's two toy poodles stay for another six months before you move, rather than spend thousands of dollars in litigation, you've achieved a modest, yet perhaps essential, victory.

Associations often take the blame for situations they can't even control. People naturally want to blame someone for their problems, and often the association is the target. At California's Leisure World, a retirement community, vacationing renters clogged the golf courses and prevented year-round residents, including owners, from enjoying their own facilities. Vacationers bent on taking advantage of the community's amenities crowded out the owners, who felt they deserved preferential treatment. The owners sued the homeowners association over the issue of renter-vacationers and won a ruling that renters couldn't receive preferential treatment over full-time residents. The homeowners association had amassed $300,000 in legal fees.

Sometimes residents want to blame homeowners associations for their problems. A Camarillo, California, resident sued his association for not providing promised security after $52,000 worth of rare coins and jewelry was stolen from his home. He lost, by the way.

Sometimes you'll find the association's actions turn your insides into an anger-generator, and you either have to fight or live with an escalated blood-pressure level. That's what happened to a Boca Raton, Florida, couple. The condo board at their trendy address sought to get rid of their dog, Lucky, a five-year-old mutt that exceeded the thirty-pound weight limit set by the board. Not so, said the owners. The board said the dog had to go, so his owners sued the board. An independent weighing saved Lucky, when he tipped the scales at between 29.4 and 31.5 pounds (he wiggled a lot), and he lived up to his name. The case was settled out of court.

Occasionally it makes sense to fight the association on its own terms and turf.

Charles and Gladys Brown did battle with their board over their potbellied pig. The board felt the pig wasn't a suitable house pet and evicted him. And although the Browns were planning to move anyway, they sued. The case is currently being prepared for trial.

None of the residents in the Browns' condo had complained about Laddie, the pig, and no one's property values had declined. The pig was neither a nuisance nor was it harming property values, and the Browns didn't understand what all the fuss was about. In fact, neighbors used to bring Laddie pig-shaped cookies at Christmas. Yet the association was adamant about enforcing its rules.

One of the easiest ways to defeat the association is to know the rules better than the board members. Often the association comes along after your house, and you may find the newfangled rules don't apply to you. That's how it worked for Rick Wilder of St. Petersburg, Florida.

For eleven years, Wilder's six-foot hedges had come between him and his neighborhood association. The hedges, because of their size, violated association rules. The association started its battle by writing letters and ended up filing a lawsuit. Wilder said that they couldn't tell him what to do because he moved in before the association even existed. He has no deed restriction. But the association kept up the harassment. Once the association noticed the hedges, it started noticing other problems with the Wilders' landscaping, as well. The association said that their grass and shrubs were growing over the back sea wall. (The association was at the ocean's edge.) And the limestone rocks in front of the house had become discolored. This would have been a laughable exercise in nit-picking, except Wilder was forced to hire a lawyer at a cost of about a thousand dollars. The homeowners association was prepared to spend even more.

This association seemed particularly busy. In fifteen years it had cited the community's 531 homeowners for violations more than 1,600 times. How could the Wilders have avoided this arbitrary assertion of power? Unfortunately, they could not have, because the association came after they did. But the lesson is clear: When you are thinking about buying into a condo, coop, or homeowners association, don't just take a look at the real estate. Thoroughly examine

•

the association board. Do they enforce the rules with the strictness of a old-fashioned schoolteacher? Does the board ignore violations, so that anarchy reigns? It's certainly appropriate for you to ask the board what kind of actions they've taken, what rule violations they ignore, whether the board has ever been sued, and whether the board has ever sued anybody.

Keep in mind that when you join an association, you aren't merely buying real estate, you're becoming a citizen of what, from your point of view, is a country. Is this country, the association, run like a dictatorship, subject to the whims of the association president and his henchmen? Is the association run benignly and flexibly? Is every single rule enforced, no matter how outmoded?

It's a well-established legal principle that laws that are not enforced regularly, and laws that are selectively enforced become unenforceable. If you can demonstrate that you are the only home-owner against whom a certain rule is being enforced, you have a good chance of winning. You may have to do some research. While *this* board may be aggressive about enforcing the rules, a previous board may have been more lax. That laxness can weigh in your favor!

Who makes the rules? What's the process for getting a rule changed? These are two important questions, along with how easily rules can be changed. Generally, there are two different kinds of rules: bylaws and board decrees. Bylaws are the most difficult to change, because they usually require that a certain percentage (50 or 66 percent most typically) of association members support the bylaw change. In many instances the bylaw changes must also occur at a meeting of a quorum of association members. Obtaining a quorum of association members at a meeting can be a very difficult task. The bylaws are the association's "constitution." Bylaws usually contain rules regarding subletting, fines, and election of officers.

Rule changes are easier. All you need is a majority of the board to support you. Rules involve issues like the size of hedges, noise, pets, maintenance, painting, and holiday decorations.

If you're not sure of your legal standing regarding a potential offense (does your parakeet qualify as a pet, or could it be construed as dinner-to-be?), remember a little conspiracy does wonders for some harmless rule bending. Ask your most immediate neighbors whether your owning a parakeet would ruffle their feathers. And while you're in their apartment, you can say, "Nice cat." You'll find that you can quickly create a conspiracy of illegal pet owners in your building.

Without the silence of your neighbors, it's hard to hide your infractions. Living in a community ruled by an association means many eyes are on you. All the time. Consider this story. When Kim Humphrey kissed her date goodnight, she thought it was a private act. Imagine her surprise days later when she saw notice on a condominium bulletin board, accusing her of breaking the regulations of the Town Square Owners Association, which governs her complex.

"Resident seen parking in circular driveway kissing and doing bad things for over 1 hour," the notice from the condominium managers read. News traveled fast, and soon teens in the community trembled, fearful that the case could mean a ban on kissing in the complex. Humphrey got a lawyer. Soon the association was backpedaling. Oops, the notice was about another resident and they issued an apology to Humphrey. They settled the case out of court.

That's the bad part of living under rule of an association: somebody is watching. Your neighbor is bound to spot your illegal pet cat sunning on the windowsill. And your neighbor sure won't miss that sailboat in the drive!

Real laws may help you in a fight against the association, as association rulings can be capricious. When their condominium president found their wooden wheelchair ramp unsightly and ordered it removed, a frail Florida couple became trapped in their home. Although the ramp had stood in use for almost eight years and none of their neighbors complained, it was removed. The couple fought to have it reinstalled on the grounds that removing it discriminated against the handicapped.

It's always a good tactic to try fighting a rule with a stronger rule. Local ordinances quiver when a federal law comes along. But be forewarned: Your association may have stricter codes than state or federal laws already in place. That is, you may have to recycle more of your trash or observe greater noise restrictions.

Sometimes the in-your-face rule violators pull off their infractions with guts and bravado of Agent 007. Board members are people too, and they have to pick and choose where they'll fight. It's no wonder that plenty of people are former association board or committee members. William Morrell, former president of a condominium association in Tarpon Springs, Florida, had a memorable

•

run-in with a neighbor at the pool. When Morrell reminded the man who was swimming with his toddler granddaughter that rules prohibited use of the pool by diapered children, the man responded by removing the diaper and putting her back in the pool. No rule violated, but the rule was changed quickly. In the meantime, the toddler had a nice swim.

## SOMETIMES CONDO ASSOCIATIONS LOSE

Sometimes associations lose—though not all that often. But here's one case where a Los Angeles, California, family went up against their homeowners association and won. When the Shermans bought two Rottweilers they simultaneously erected a six-foot-high block wall between themselves and their neighbors "for the safety of our neighbors' children," John Sherman said. Unfortunately, the rules of the homeowners association, representing houses valued at $1 million and more, required members to get permission before erecting fences of any kind. The homeowners association's board objected to the fence on two grounds: first, the Shermans hadn't obtained permission to build it; and second, it was "visible and ugly, and we didn't want to set a precedent," according to one board member.

Before the Shermans and the homeowners association slugged it out in court, the Shermans offered to landscape the wall. The association said "No," the favorite word of homeowners associations.

But by this time the homeowners association had locked horns with the Shermans. The association didn't want any wall, and besides, they didn't like the way *that* wall (all ninety feet of it) looked: no compromise. The Shermans' next-door neighbors, who originally complained about the wall, wrote the association just before the case went to court: "Frankly, we are tired of the whole situation and want it ended. If the status of the wall rested on us, then it should have been settled between us without expensive legal opinions." But the association wouldn't bend.

When the battle ended, the Shermans were allowed to keep their wall and the association had to pay them $150,000 for their legal fees. All five board members resigned after the court made the association pay the fee.

Bad blood remains between the Shermans and other members of the homeowners association. The Shermans wrote all members of the association, saying, "In retrospect, we wish we never had to go through the misery of this lawsuit that pitted neighbor against neighbor." The letter also reminded association members that they would have to pay the $150,000.

What's the lesson? There are plenty of lessons, depending on your point of view. The most important is that homeowners associations don't always win. In the Shermans' case, an impenetrable barrier was necessary. Rottweilers are good at jumping. An ordinary fence—the kind the Shermans already had, with bars five inches apart—wouldn't have sufficed because any child who put his fingers through the fence and said, "nice doggy, doggy" could have lost a digit, and the Shermans would have been liable. Had the association banned dogs, then the Shermans would have been out of luck, but because of the way the rule was written, the association lost.

It's become my opinion, after observing dozens of neighbor squabbles, that there is a short list of things you should avoid in life: (1) getting stung by a whole colony of bees, (2) flying in hurricanes and tornadoes, (3) living under the rule of an inflexible homeowners association, especially one without a sense of humor.

Many families *want* to become part of homeowners associations. (Many have no choice, really, because the only way they can live in a particular place is to move into a community with a homeowners association.) People long for a feeling of community that they believe that a homeowners association will give them. People long for the stability, the preservation of the status quo that these associations are so famous for protecting.

Frankly, it's hard for me to fathom why somebody would *want* to live in a place that has more rules than their state and city. Most localities have regulations regarding signage—what kind of advertising you are permitted to display. That kind of regulation makes sense. But some homeowners associations have regulations regarding what, if any, ornaments you can place on your door.

This fits into the hard-to-believe-but-true category. A resident of a Fairfax, Virginia, community was sued by his homeowners association because he placed a Christmas wreath on his front door. The association didn't permit any kind of object on front doors unless prior approval was granted. Sorry, Santa, you'll have to skip this homeowners association.

Another association member couldn't keep his van in the association's parking area, even though he owned the space and there was no prohibition against vans. The reason? The hardworking American's van had a business name and phone number painted on the side of the van. You see, it was the man's only car, and his most important tool for earning money. The van wasn't used for commercial purposes on the association's property; it was just parked there. But the signage rules prevailed.

Homeowners associations vote, and when votes are taken, sides are taken, and when sides are taken, neighbors must disagree. Sometimes these disagreements are minor; sometimes they lead to war. Witness what occurred in a Sherman Oaks, California, association. In 1992 the association filed a lawsuit against the developer alleging shoddy construction, negligence, and fraud in the development of the townhouses in the complex. Cracks in concrete, faulty plumbing, electrical wiring not to code, and a host of other problems formed the basis of a $25 million lawsuit.

So where's the problem?

The problem is that only half of the 214 owners in the association felt that the lawsuit should move forward. The other half felt that things weren't so bad and all a lawsuit would do would be to lower property values and prevent owners from selling their homes. How bad was the dispute? The camps were so bitterly divided that when somebody from the developer's company met with a resident, doors sprang open and ears perked up, as if the Devil himself were dashing through the hall. At an association board meeting, one homeowner punched another in the nose. Somebody from the developer's side obtained a copy of the association president's credit report and circulated it anonymously. Another resident's diary was faked with obscene entries and posted on the communal bulletin board. Stay tuned—the fight's not over yet.

But when you win, you sometimes win big. And that's the dream that fuels most legal battles with associations. People are so convinced they are right that they just can't give up. Occasionally they actually are right.

When a water leak from an upstairs unit damaged his bathroom wallpaper, Nat Jeppson, who owned the unit, asked his association to make up the $135 difference between the cost of the repair and his insurance reimbursement. When the condo association refused, Jeppson sued. After a two-year legal battle, the courts ruled in favor of the unit owner and ordered the association to pay all legal fees. In the end, the association was liable for thirty thousand dollars.

Lawsuits fly so fast in real estate that even associations seek protection. A California homeowners association sought guidance on its own covenants, conditions, and restrictions from the Orange County Superior Court! When two homeowners objected to a third neighbor's building of a covered patio, they appealed to the homeowners association to prohibit the construction. But the association saw itself in a bind. The builders might sue them if they ruled for the obstructionists, and the obstructionists might sue them if the patio was permitted. "Should we approve or deny the construction permit?" they asked the court. Approve was the answer.

## NEIGHBOR VS. NEIGHBOR

So what do you do when you live in a condo, have noisy neighbors, and the condo board won't do anything about it? You know the situation: There's a pounding, pounding, pounding going on upstairs. A basketball, perhaps, or maybe the people upstairs testing how various household appliances stand stress. When one Chicago condo dweller was experiencing just this sort of noise, he appealed to the condo board, which graciously offered to do nothing. The upstairs neighbor was a bit more helpful, offering suggestions as to what the downstairs neighbor could do with a broom handle.

What's the solution when your condo board won't help? There are two approaches you can take. First, a nuisance lawsuit, though this is an expensive and time-consuming option. (More on nuisance lawsuits in the chapter on special strategies.) A second option is to invite the condo board, or part of the board, to your apartment for a listen. In many circumstances, the power-in-authority, in this case the condo board, simply doesn't believe you. They think you're either a liar (that's what the paranoid board members believe) or you're a lunatic (that's what the remaining board members believe). So bake some cookies, have some cold soda or beer ready, and be ready to demonstrate to the board that you're not a stodgy crank. If the noise is loud enough, they'll hear it. (They might support your side just to avoid having to join you at 2 A.M.)

While builders are often prohibited from installing terrazzo or tile floors throughout a condo, residents are not. When their upstairs neighbors installed a terrazzo floor, the downstairs dwellers in a Boca Raton, Florida, condo were plagued by noise: high heels on the floor after a night on the town; the sound of furniture being moved. But the culprits were unmoved by their neighbors' pleas for quiet. In the end, the neighbors had to appeal to their condo board. Most condominium bylaws rule that no apartment owner can create noises and nuisances to interfere with the rights of other residents or annoy them. In fact, a landmark case, the Baum vs. Coronado case, which involved terrazzo flooring, gave injunctive relief from the noise of upstairs neighbors.

•••••••••••••••••••••••••••••••••••••••••••••••••••••••••••••••••••••••

### FIGHTING THE POWER

Trade in your chits. Agree to cancel your daughter's drum lessons if your neighbors will support you in your fight against the association.

Get your neighbors on your side.

Locate neighbors who don't like the noisemaking neighbor.

Don't be too fast to turn in your neighbor for an infraction. You might want to trade one of his misbehaviors for one of yours.

•••••••••••••••••••••••••••••••••••••••••••••••••••••••••••••••••••••••

## MONEY MATTERS

Associations often have the upper hand in battles because they have bigger billfolds than individual members. Many associations can levy fines. They may be able to take their fines out of your association dues. Then you've defaulted on your dues, and they come after your home. That's what happened to Mark Kompa.

Santa Ana, California, attorney Kompa was hit with a volley of fines from his homeowners association when he failed to plant ground cover on a slope. Initially he was fined $150, which he refused to pay. Subsequent fines swelled the amount to $3,493.91. When Kompa demanded to see the managing company's accounting records, they refused and referred his case to a foreclosure specialist, who proposed to sell the home at an auction to pay off the fine.

It's expensive to buck the system.

Ask Dotti Ryan. Even the most lazy of teenagers could have agreed to mow Ryan's lawn. It's tiny. But her failure to mow her tiny lawn may have caused her to lose her home. When the association decided her lawn was unsightly, they had professional gardeners attend to it and repair three sprinklers—and sent her the bill for five hundred dollars.

When she refused to pay, the association used her monthly dues to pay the gardener, and so her dues became delinquent and opened her up to foreclosure action. Ryan would have been happy to settle for a thousand dollars to have the lien removed so she could sell the property.

When an association attacks, it's often with a swift ferocity. Often there's no defense, or victory comes at great personal and emotional expense. Residents contend that overzealous association board members prowl the neighborhood looking for violations. Sometimes that's the case, but too often the people turning you in are your neighbors, and that hurts—especially when you think you're doing something for the good of everyone.

When a Philadelphia family built a backyard fence to prevent their children from falling over a ledge there, the structure was quickly discovered and ordered removed. A court upheld the judgment, and the fence had to go. No matter that the fence protected all neighborhood children: it was more important to keep up appearances.

There are defenses against excessive fines. Suing—or threatening to sue—is one strategy. You can take advantage of the fact that many association members don't want their association spending money on a lawsuit. If the association thinks that you are serious and that you are going to cost them more in legal expenses than they could acquire in fines, they may back off. Or at least settle.

Even if the association board is intransigent, there probably are association members who feel that the monthly dues are too high. When these neighbors realize that you're going to cost the condo $5,000, $10,000 or more, they may ask the board to back off. You may have to work hard to identify those frugal association members, but the effort will be worth it.

It's hard to live under all the different regulations that come with living in a community ruled by an association. Sometimes residents living under the rules of conformity go a little nuts. Although they know they shouldn't go against the rules, something inside—rebellion, excess energy, or childishness—eggs them on.

That's what happened to Bob Lloyd when he painted his home a light shade of purple, while all his neighbors' homes were beige and gray. He knew the homeowners association strictly enforced its aesthetic standards, standards he agreed to when he moved into the development near Seattle. The trim he painted a deep purple, which contrasted nicely with the bit of teal around the windows. The association nearly blew a gasket.

After years of following the rules, Lloyd had broken out, and he wasn't going to back down. He fought all the way to the King County Superior Court.

The court ordered him to follow the rules. In the end, facing the twin threats—of imprisonment, for failing to follow the judge's instructions, and fines of up to $2,000 a day—Lloyd repainted his home. But he and his family didn't give in easily. The association had to drag Lloyd kicking and screaming before he relented. Before they repainted, Lloyd and his wife had their wages and checking account garnisheed and a lien put on their house.

Lloyd seemed unable to help himself. He knew the rules, but he rebelled. With an estimated one in eight people living in homes ruled by associations, this sort of rebellion is on the increase. People are up in arms against dictatorial boards and inconsistent rule enforcement. Who can blame them? (Residents who don't like change, that's who.)

Associations can be sticklers for petty details. In Reston, Virginia, the association told Betsy Santos to rip up her seven-thousand-dollar deck because its rail was slanted instead of straight. And in nearby Silver Spring, Maryland, they told Ron Appel to tear up his concrete driveway because it was three inches too wide. Sometimes it's easier to move than to fight.

Some people just don't read the rules closely before they move in. Seduced by the pools, lakes, or other amenities offered by the community, they put off reading the thick, legalistic association rules and regulations. They prefer to get their information in smaller quantities, like when the homeowners association sends a letter pointing out a violation and levying a fine. But there's a trade-off in living in a managed community; on the one hand there is enforced homogeneity, and on the other hand, each family's property values are tied to what the association does. Residents trade off some of their individual rights for community ones.

Sometimes people choose to ignore the most obvious rules when they secure a mortgage. Young couples who have children or are planning to have children move into communities designated for senior citizens only. A community for residents over age forty-five has to threaten to kick out people under the age limit. Even if you manage to work around the problem on some technical issue, you're still living in a place where the people don't want you. If you want to make a statement by moving into a community where you don't belong, where there are more hospitals than playgrounds and more shuffleboard courts than swing sets, then you do so at risk.

Fighting the association even on the pettiest of issues is often expensive and sometimes emotionally and financially crippling. One homeowner fought his condo association for the right to park his recreational vehicle next to his unit. He lost and was ordered to pay the association's legal fees. His bill—$37,000.

•••••••••••••••••••••••••••••••••••••••••••••••••••••••••••••••••••

## A BLOW TO THE WALLET

Pick your battles carefully. If your neighbors are united against you, it may be easier for you to move.

Pay your fines. A court may award them back to you if you win a suit, but if you lose the case, you may lose your home if the association takes the fines out of your monthly dues and marks your payments delinquent.

•••••••••••••••••••••••••••••••••••••••••••••••••••••••••••••••••••

## DIRTY POLITICS

There are several ways of looking at people. There are tall people and small people. There are old people and young people. There are wise people and wisdom-challenged people. There are dog owners and there are dog nonowners. But, most of all, there are pro–speed-bump people and anti–speed-bump people.

Well, maybe that's not the number one issue among most associations, but it was a key issue among several residents of the Silver

Time Association in Los Angeles, California. Citing the potential legal liabilities of having small children or animals squashed by speeding motorists, the pro–speed-bump faction mustered considerable moral clout. The pro-bumpers pointed to other associations that had posted 15 mph signs along with bumps. The speed bumps cost only four hundred dollars each, so the cost compared to the potential cost of a lawsuit was minuscule.

But something smelled fishy to one member of the Silver Time board. Nobody had ever met any of the pro-bumpers; they had just heard from them by letter. After a brief investigation, the board discovered that the pro-bumpers consisted of a single homeowner who lived at the bottom of a hill.

That's how things happen sometimes. Because of the general apathy of association members, the enthusiastic few can control things for the many. And the few get power happy. (Keep that in mind when you need to rally support for your pet project.)

Byron Thomas resides in a planned community in Reston, Virginia, just outside of Washington, D.C. He simply wanted to know how his association dues were spent.

With nearly one hundred permanent employees and a $7 million budget, the Reston Association charged Thomas about $300 a year, nearly double what he had paid when he moved to Reston in 1975. "Where does all that money go?" he wondered. When he asked to see payroll information, the association refused, and he had to sue to find out. Associations, depending on their bylaws, don't have to reveal their inner working to their subjects . . . er, residents.

One of the biggest lessons of this chapter is that it pays to get involved with your board. In most cases, that's pretty easy. In rare circumstances, board members have things set up to ensure their position and power. To alter this, your first fight will be changing election procedures. Find out how your board gets elected and who may vote. Who selects the candidates? In many cases, board members abuse their privileges of office to ensure their reelection. Association newsletters feature the candidates in office, not the challengers. Challengers are unfairly represented in articles and don't get a chance to respond.

Voting procedures may also be set up to favor incumbent board members. Often these board members rule by proxy—that is, members of the association may appoint someone to vote for them at elections. They typically give their votes to the board members. Find out who can cast a proxy—any unit owner or just officers and board members? Because of life's hustle and bustle and ordinary apathy, proxies are often abused. People use the process to control election results.

Are people so petty that they'll cheat at a condo board election? Ask Ware Bingham, a board member at Houghton Condominium Association near Chicago. He's been engaged in a lawsuit against the board to force it to conduct fair elections. He noted that the board hadn't changed in seven years—kept the same year in and year out by the proxy procedure that allowed the board to control the election. The closed process made change difficult.

The board controlled everything. Notices of elections and proxies were prepared and mailed with association funds, an unfair advantage when the condo is a large one. A judge agreed that the current proxy ballot was against the law but ruled against Bingham on some other election points. Bingham appealed. He kept alive a fight over procedural matters, one most people wouldn't have the patience to deal with. He's steered the future of his condo. It's not a sexy issue, not one that most people even understand or care about. But it's a noble battle.

Still, his board played dirty. While Bingham said his legal fees have been about two thousand dollars, the board circulated rumors that their legal fees have been in excess of twenty thousand dollars. Naturally, his neighbors are pressuring Bingham to give up his battle.

So if your board isn't one of the types that welcomes participation, you may have quite a battle ahead.

••••••••••••••••••••••••••••••••••••••••••••••••••••••••••••••••

## THE GOOD FIGHT

Look into board election policy. If the rules set things up so that the same board retains power year after year, work to shake things up. Make the board members want to call you "madam" or "sir."

••••••••••••••••••••••••••••••••••••••••••••••••••••••••••••••••

•

# 3

# Developer Neighbors and Obstructionist Neighbors

### Situation 1

You're minding your own business, adding a deck to the house, when an inspector appears. He says there's been a complaint and wants to see the permits. Trouble is, you don't exactly have them (since you're doing the work yourself). How did the inspector find out? Could it be because the neighbor across the street didn't like the color of the wood you selected?

### Situation 2

*You can hardly believe she's doing it again.* Another addition? First she renovated the entire inside of the house; the work lasted a year. Next, she screened in the front porch. Then she landscaped. Not too long after, she added a shed in the backyard. And now, she seems to be adding solar panels to the roof. You haven't been able to sleep in for about three years. Will it ever end?

Here we have the two major types of neighbors. The ones who endlessly hammer away at their fortresses and the ones who can't bear the noise and inconvenience involved in your getting the work done.

## INSTANT (AND ILLEGAL) PROJECTS AND BUSY BEAVERS

Sometimes it happens like this. You're away for the weekend. Before you leave, you check the security and safety of your home: newspaper stopped; windows locked; lights on timer; heater turned down; cat food put out; everything set.

After your perfect weekend in the country you return and find that, as you drive down the block approaching your house, something looks amiss. That something is a rather large, ugly deck your neighbor erected over the weekend. An unsightly structure that casts a dark shadow on your garden. How was the deck erected so quickly?

Perhaps the more important question is: *Why* was the deck erected so quickly? The answer often is, "Because it is illegal." No permit, no zoning variance, none of the usual paperwork that ordinarily needs to accompany a structure in a residential neighborhood. That's why the deck grew so fast, and that happens to be why its spontaneous generation took place while you were away for the weekend.

So now what are you going to do? Obviously, if the deck went up secretly, like a clandestine military project during wartime, then this is war. There's no reason why you shouldn't approach your neighbor with sad eyes and talk about your sun-starved flower garden, but there's very little chance that he's going to tear down the structure. If you can't be happy with some sort of compromise—and compromise may be the best you can get—like removing part of the deck, then you should consider embarking on the arduous path that will likely destroy your neighborly relations: forcing the structure down.

The only body with the power to force an illegal structure down is the government. Do a little research to find out what local laws the structure violates. Then send your neighbor a registered letter laying out his offenses.

You then need to set up your case carefully. The best first step—take a photograph. Photos are often stronger that mere words. With a picture, government officials can see the outrageous violation that you're talking about. (Somebody from your local zoning or permits office will eventually visit the site, but not everybody involved in the case will.)

Careful planning before taking pictures of illegal buildings can be decisively rewarding. Have your smallest child stand in front of the structure (or borrow a small child). Putting a twenty-seven-inch person in front of a deck or garage makes the structure seem colossal, an imposing building that any rational person would agree is big beyond reason. Try it—you have nothing to lose. Also, see if you can find a picture of the same area before the structure went up. The before-and-after shots really help make the case.

Unfortunately, it's tough to do anything about illegal structures once they're up. Government sanctions work at a glacial pace, leaving you stuck looking at an offensive architectural creation. Even then, the government may just fine your neighbor without demanding the structure's removal. But that doesn't mean you shouldn't find out if the structure is illegal.

When Sid Ganish's neighbors grew tired of his seemingly endless renovations, they complained to the city. In response, Irvine, California, now has a new law on its books, the Residence Remodeling Law, which requires that all remodeling work on a house be completed within a year of the issuance of a work permit.

If the only offense you can find is the lack of a building permit, maybe you'll want to consider your options before you act. If you snitch on your neighbor and he's levied a fine, then how will you persuade him to do anything to ameliorate the damage he's caused? A lattice-covered wall with morning glories or honeysuckle climbing it can lessen the impact of a new garage. Maybe you can paint a mural on the offending wall. Perhaps your neighbor will look the other way while you build your own illegal structure.

•  •  •

## IT TAKES TWO TO TANGO

Remember, practically everything you do to your house affects your neighbors. Building a back deck? The deck alone is going to make your neighbor feel claustrophobic, not to mention the parties and dinners you plan to have out there. Before you build, consider its impact on your neighbor. I'm not saying that you shouldn't build because your neighbor objects. What I am saying is that you should modify your grand schemes to take your neighbor's life into account.

If you even thinking of building an addition without a permit, zoning variance, or whatever permission you require—don't. It's one thing to build close to your neighbor's house if the structure is legal. If it's legal, your neighbor has to live with what you do. If it's illegal and your neighbor doesn't like what you've built, then you've given your neighbor fuel, ammunition, a missile launcher—a whole arsenal—to fight what you've done.

If you've just moved and are thinking about renovating, let your neighbors see your plans ahead of time. It's a bad idea to join a neighborhood, then immediately sour any potentially good relationship you might have with your neighbors.

If you feel that you can live with that illegal structure, now is the time to announce *your* plans for renovations to your neighbor. How can he object now?

What if your neighbor puts up a structure in clear violation of the law? I think that most of the time lawsuits do little good and much harm. But there are times when they work quickly and efficiently. An Arkansas woman irked her neighbors when she moved a mobile home onto her property, although her deed specifically forbade it. She scurried to cover her acts. First, she had the wheels removed and placed the home atop concrete footings. To further disguise it, she put in a septic tank, built a front porch, a carport, and a storage room. To top it off, she built a stone wall in front of the home at the base. All told, she spent about five thousand dollars. Her neighbors complained to the courts because it was too late to do anything about the home after all that construction. Was it still a mobile home? Expert witnesses testified it was a mobile home. In the end, the woman sealed her own fate. She registered it with the Department of Finance and Administration Registration as a mobile home for tax purposes. She insured it as a mobile home. And when she bought it, she went to Quality Mobile Homes. Move it along, lady, the courts said. Chalk one up for the neighbors!

You can't object too successfully to your neighbor's projects if you are a high-stakes developer. Did you put in a central air-conditioning condenser too close to your neighbor's house, and did your neighbor kindly ask you to put it somewhere else? If he did, and you didn't, then you can just about forget having any of your requests honored. Did you install a basketball hoop underneath your neighbor's bedroom window? Then you're going to have a hard time convincing your neighbor not to work on his construction projects all weekend long.

• • • • • • • • • • • • • • • • • • • • • • • • • • • • • • • • • • • • • • • • •

## UNDEVELOPING

Look for signs of impending construction: a growing pile of tools and supplies, permits, or clearing of trees and underbrush. Then be nosy. Find out what your neighbor is planning.

If the work is complete and done without proper notification, research local ordinances to see if your neighbor has broken any laws. Visit and let your neighbor know his outlaw status—and that you're willing to overlook a few things if he will make a few changes.

• • • • • • • • • • • • • • • • • • • • • • • • • • • • • • • • • • • • • • • • • •

## LIMITED VISTAS

When a neighbor's new addition blocks your view, it's usually a declaration of neighbor war. A lot of things are true of human nature, but perhaps the truest is that if your neighbor designs a structure that ruins the view you paid so dearly for, there's bound to be trouble.

Take the case of the Santa Monica homeowner, Brian Swain, who tried to build an addition to his house, which bordered a homeowners association building. After four years of legal jousting, Swain was forced to tear down his addition because it blocked the homeowners association's magnificent views of the Santa Monica Canyon and Pacific Ocean. It was a vicious battle. First the homeowners association got a stop-work order issued; then Swain violated the stop-work order; the association finally got a court order to have him stop.

The association and homeowner, needless to add, were not fast friends; nor were they good neighbors. But what ultimately enabled the association to claim victory wasn't the fact that a vista would be lost, but a zoning ordinance prohibited any building from being constructed higher than street level, which this addition would have been. (Swain, by the way, was also involved in a losing lawsuit with his next-door neighbor. Swain built an addition that took over part of a driveway easement that he and his neighbor shared. It turned out to be a big lawsuit, with Swain ending up having to sell his house. The neighbor said of the victory, "I feel great. This is like recovering from an affliction.")

But I digress.

This story brings up two important points regarding neighbor battles over scenic views. Although the citizens won their battle to get the view back, views are not guaranteed anywhere by law. Your wonderful vista can be blocked. Unless your house is on the edge of a cliff, or unless zoning or other regulations prohibit building, there's a chance that what you see could disappear. Sims did not lose on the view issue; he lost because he had violated zoning ordinances.

Furthermore, if a neighbor has a history of building obnoxious additions, you can be pretty sure he'll do it again. And again. Once a developer, always a developer. Neighbors of this type have little or no interest in their neighbors' wishes and dreams. Beware of them.

Still, you may be able to frustrate your neighbor's creative urges long enough for you to sell your home and move far away.

Organize your neighbors to oppose the construction. Research the project to see what you can find that's illegal. Each infraction will cost your neighbor time, and who knows, maybe the cumulative frustration will cause him or her to stop the current project. At any rate, while construction is halted, you can use the opportunity to sell your home.

Here's another case fought over views and won on a height restriction. In Huntington Beach, California, Ali Imanitah built a custom three-story home that blocked his neighbors' view of the ocean. Neighbors had opposed construction since the first brick was laid.

·

More than a hundred of them signed a petition opposing it, although many objected more to its size and appearance than to its view-obstructing position.

Furious at the new monstrosity, they sued the city for allowing the construction. First the case went to Orange County superior court, then to the state appellate court. After years of litigation, the neighbors won when the city council ordered Imanitah to remove the top floor of the house because it violated a local height limitation, not because the house blocked anyone's ocean view. But it doesn't end there; Imanitah is suing the city for allowing him to build originally.

What about other eyesores your neighbor erects? You get up, fix that first cup of coffee, and sit down to enjoy it while you look out the window. Staring straight back at you is a brand-spankin'-new satellite dish. Surprise. Perhaps it's perfectly legal. Maybe not.

Sometimes they're erected even though local covenants forbid them. And sometimes it's hard to know what the local ordinance is trying to prevent. That's what happened in a Clive, Iowa, development. The development included a restriction against extension towers—but not dishes—in its rules. So when a couple moved into the development and installed a satellite dish, the homeowners association came after them. The couple professed innocence. They had a dish, not an extension tower. In the spirit of compromise, they traded their ten-foot dish for a seven-foot one. In the development, where homes sell upward of $350,000, the dish wasn't too popular, no matter the size. The case hadn't been decided as this book went to print.

If your neighbor's satellite dish (or barbecue pit, swimming pool, ugly utilitarian structure, clothesline, antenna, or tennis court) gives you a headache every time you look at it, you may get some relief by building a fence. If you build it on the property line, maybe your neighbor will split the cost. At any rate, you'll need permission to build a fence there, and you may want to sign an agreement that gives you the right to take care of the fence and lays out any financial agreements about its upkeep. Your neighbor may agree to build or plant something that improves your view somewhat. You can always build a fence one inch into your property; for that you don't need your neighbor's permission, just the city's. If you do build a fence inside your property line, make sure that everyone knows you've done it, so over the years the size of your property doesn't decrease by one inch on that side.

Forcing someone to tear down a structure after it's been built is a rough legal and regulatory road, even if the structure was built illegally, so you need to be forever on the watch for construction in the neighborhood. Keep an eye out for surveyors, tree clearing in your neighbor's yard, trucks that read "general contractor" on the side.

In an emergency, stop-work orders are effective. But only in an emergency. (Beware, also, neighbors who just shrug them aside.)

It's best to try reasoning with your neighbor before he's invested money, and most of all, emotion in the addition or new construction. If your neighbor doesn't want to consider compromise in the name of neighborly harmony, it's time to research legal means to halt or change the nature of the construction.

If local ordinances don't protect your view, you have little recourse. Of course you can sue. That's what actor Alec Baldwin's* neighbors did when he built a second-floor addition to his home in Amagansett, New York. His neighbors Lee and Kate Lewyn sued, although Baldwin hadn't violated any laws and had followed through completely on his permit process. Still, the Lewyns were angry because the Baldwin structure had blocked their last remaining bit of ocean vista, and when they lost their suit, they appealed. It's unlikely that the case will be overturned, since Baldwin broke no law. In fact, Baldwin's attorney found several zoning violations on the Lewyns' property, and in addition to their court costs, they had to pay for their zoning violations.

Alternatively, if you're the one with the offending structure, take aggressive action to terminate conflict before your neighbors get angry. If you have an objectionable satellite dish, offer to share reception. Now that's a great deal!

• • • • • • • • • • • • • • • • • • • • • • • • • • • • • • • • • • • • • • • • • • •

## PRETTY SIGHTS

Plant fast-growing evergreens to block the view of an offending structure.

See if you can share reception from an antenna or satellite dish.

• • • • • • • • • • • • • • • • • • • • • • • • • • • • • • • • • • • • • • • • • • •

* Real name

## THE INCREDIBLE GROWING PROJECT

Imagine (if you can) living next door to Millard (Mickey) Ryland,* president of the Gap, Inc. He was redoing his house. A commonplace occurrence, right? But Ryland lives along the Presidio Wall in San Francisco.

Determined to restore his nearly eighty-year-old home to its previous glory, Ryland worked on it for over two years. His vision meant more than replacing a few windows. First, he took the house down to the studs; then he rebuilt it.

His project has involved cranes, cement trucks, timber trucks. Neighbors' homes were filled with the dust and debris blowing in from the construction. One neighbor counted twenty-five trucks and cars of people involved in the construction. These people have left trash, from stray gum wrappers to plastic coverings blowing off timber loads.

Still, the neighbors can't say they weren't warned. Before the work started, Ryland had them over to see his three-story home and to review the plans. He changed the work start time from 7 to 8:30 A.M. in response to their objections. Every night, the workers cleaned up the street. Still, people were inconvenienced by the project. And then there was the parking problem, and the necessary noise.

It's unlikely Ryland will take on another project like this one. You can't fault him for not trying to do the right thing. You can follow his example and improve upon it. Make sure your workers are neatniks. Make sure no wood chips blow into your neighbor's yard, no fast-food bags fall on their lawn. Also make sure your workers observe noise ordinances. A certain amount of noise comes with the work, but you should make sure it happens at a time tolerable to your neighbors. If you know your neighbor's baby naps at 2 P.M., hold up the electric band saw until four in the afternoon. Even if they don't nap, it would be nice to warn neighbors, so they don't invite guests that day.

Go out of your way to be helpful. If you can afford it, have work start late in the day. Eschew construction on weekends.

Obey the local labor laws. If you can't control your workers because the jobs are subcontracted, threaten to withhold payment if your demands aren't met.

* Real name

When it's all over, invite all the neighbors to a party to celebrate your complete renovations. You and your renovation will be remembered more fondly because of it.

But considerate neighbors, like Ryland, are the nice guys. What if your neighbor isn't?

Oftentimes your only recourse is to try and stop construction. But this is a monumental task. Just ask Peter Winston. He spent over $300,000 trying to stop a renovation. Winston's lovely home was perched atop a lonely hill overlooking the ocean. Or it was lonely until Barry Callahan came along. Callahan wanted to build a new home, a scant ten feet away from the Winston residence—a new home that would rise 50 feet and occupy 4,400 square feet. So Winston fought the best way he knew. He tried lobbying city council members for their support, and he has gone to court several times to stop the Callahan construction. And he is suing the homeowners group that approved Callahan's project. He attended so many Malibu city council meetings that he should be made an honorary member. He sent them letters nearly every day. Winston complained that the construction workers harassed him and his family. He worried that the Callahans' maid would have a prime view of the Winston Jacuzzi and spa.

Although Winston has sunk $300,000 into this suit, it's not his first. He has also sued a neighbor who was trying to subdivide her property. He once threatened to sue a landowner when a rock rolled down a hill and dented his garage. After Mrs. Winston alleged Callahan threatened her husband, Winston got a court order that prohibited Callahan from going within one hundred yards of the Winstons. (Could this prevent him from living in the home ten feet away or would he have to keep out of certain rooms?) Winston also had round-the-clock personal security from Wells Fargo.

The point is, some people just aren't considerate. It's hard to understand why anyone would choose to build so close to a neighbor when there were other options or why a middle-ground solution couldn't be reached.

Certain renovations are simply eyesores. That's what some Hollywood neighbors thought about Madonna's* changes to her mansion. When she bought the Hollywood landmark Castillo del Lago estate in 1993, she immediately painted the white mansion a

---

* Among the very few real names used in this book.

startling dark russet with canary-yellow stripes. Neighbors were disgusted. (Just like her neighbors in Miami when she hung black canvas sheets on the front gates to her estate to ensure her privacy.) However outraged and shocked they might be, her neighbors had as much hope of getting Madonna to change her decorating scheme as of getting her to write 1960s-style folk lyrics.

Most neighbors aren't Madonna, so it's sometimes useful to try to pressure a neighbor into changing his structure.

Occasionally development complaints take on an absurdist twist as they did when a West Hollywood, California man decided six of his neighbors had conspired together to influence the city to deny him a building permit. After exchanging angry words with them, he proceeded to stare at them so much whenever he encountered them that they called a sheriff.

• • • • • • • • • • • • • • • • • • • • • • • • • • • • • • • • • • • • • • • • • • • • • •

## CONTROLLING YOUR LIFE

If workers are awakening you too early, find out the permissible work hours for construction. In the absence of law on your side, see if your neighbor will have the workers come later, simply out of consideration. This is especially effective if he's going to need your approval for some phase of the project.

Alternatively, the workers may be violating noise ordinances.

If they're parked illegally, demand the city take action.

Have the city check out the permits for the site.

Be reasonable if your neighbor is reasonable.

• • • • • • • • • • • • • • • • • • • • • • • • • • • • • • • • • • • • • • • • • • • • • •

## THE END RUN: AVOIDING THE OBSTRUCTIONISTS

What do you do when your neighbor is a historic preservationist in a neighborhood that's not a historic one? He opposes every project you propose. He bugs you every time you so much as plant a bulb.

You beat these people by doing all your work by the book. Make sure your permits are in order. If they're not, you may be forced to restore your home to its original status or you'll be paying fines until the day you die.

No matter the size of your project, let your neighbor know what you'll be doing. Not only is this courteous, but many jurisdictions require neighbor notification when major renovations are about to occur. If your neighbor has a gripe, listen. And understand. Then make him feel like a zealous busybody: "None of the other neighbors thought a Ferris wheel would be a disturbance." At any rate, just posting your construction permit in the window isn't enough notice. Neither is a letter. Your neighbor deserves a face-to-face explanation of your renovation. It's going to affect him as well as you. Besides, your neighbor may have some worthwhile suggestions. If you know to plan around his solar panel, you won't be rebuilding to accommodate it at the end of the project. There: with one meeting, you've made your neighbors happy, and they'll pass you on any required neighbor review.

When you aren't honest about what you're doing, the neighbors suspect the worst motives for your sneakiness. That's what happened in New Haven, Connecticut. A secretive renovation blew up into a giant court case and then turned around and ate the plaintiffs.

A group of neighbors tried to oppose a neighborhood remodeling job on zoning grounds in state court. Now the U.S. Justice Department is investigating them for discrimination against the disabled. The case began when Marjorie Schneider wanted to remodel a mansion to accommodate her and her adopted and foster children. The neighborhood, home to a U.S. congresswoman (who is not involved in the suit), is one of New Haven's most exclusive.

Albertus Magnus College, a small Catholic liberal arts college, started the problem with their secretive sale to the woman. They had used the mansion, as well as the one next door, as a dormitory for nearly twenty-five years. Schneider wanted the twenty-one-room home for herself, her grown son and daughter-in-law, her six adopted children, and the four foster children whom she's in the process of adopting. She got a state grant to buy and renovate the house, without disclosing her intentions to her neighbors.

The neighborhood association and some single neighbors sought to block Schneider from moving into the home because the neighborhood is zoned as a single-family residential zone, and they felt Schneider's group didn't meet the definition of family. The neighbors didn't pursue the suit far, and quickly dropped the charges before the legal wheels really got rolling—but not before they had attracted some notice.

•

By then the state Office of Protection and Advocacy for Persons with Disabilities was involved on Schneider's side, and Schneider's attorney informed the court that all ten of the children are black or Latino and all have a disability. After some legal maneuverings on both sides, the U.S. Justice Department filed a brief in support of Schneider. The neighborhood association sensed trouble and withdrew the complaint. But by then the great machinery of the Justice Department was creaking along and not ready to stop. It began an investigation into discrimination on the part of the opposing neighbors. It sent letters to some individuals involved in the suit and the neighborhood association, threatening to sue for violation of the federal Fair Housing Act. In Schneider's name, they demanded compensation for attorneys' fees of about $33,000, a small amount of damages for emotional distress, and civil penalties of $25,000 or more.

The whole battle might have been avoided had Schneider been open about what she was doing, but her secretive actions roused neighbor curiosity. If her project wasn't bad, why was she so quiet about it? they wondered. This case proves that some of your neighbors will suspect the worst. Dig a fish pond, and they'll be convinced you're burying bodies. Eliminate speculation by telling your neighbors what you're up to. (Unless you really want to keep your project a secret.)

If your neighbors won't give their permission for your major renovation, let them know you'll remember the favor when they want to renovate.

Here's a story that's both sad and hard to believe. But it demonstrates how shortsighted and mean some neighbors can be:

*We're Oakland firestorm victims, and have begun rebuilding. Now, if we had decided to build a home in a neighborhood that had been established for twenty-some years, I might understand about the fuss and muss. But, nothing remained within three blocks of our place (to the west) and twenty blocks to the east after the '91 fire.*

*That said, our neighbors have been extremely fussy about our reconstruction—the two who are living in their recently reconstructed homes, and the two who are still in the reconstruction process themselves!*

*One has called the police several times because earthmoving equipment narrows the roadway, and he can't swing his Mercedes into his garage without turning around first.*

*We have a road-blockage permit, and the police come, laugh, and leave each time. The other has called the city several times because he envisions a Malibu-style mudslide resulting from our reconstruction, and this neighbor wants us to wait until summer. The city comes out, sees that we're complying with the "special conditions" imposed on our permit for winter grading, and leaves, only to be called out again in a couple of days. Now, our neighbor wants us to pay for additional drainage on his lot, because the water from the spring in his backyard (which has been there since the thirties anyway) must be traversing our lot underground. (Yes, our soils report shows water-bearing sandstone at eighteen feet of depth—so what?)*

*I'm glad he hasn't so far thought about the magma that must be deep under my property. He'll have the Mount Pinatubo guys suing me soon, for sure!*

*The next-door neighbors, who, without asking, built a temporary platform in our yard during their construction, eroding our hillside, are now complaining that our construction makes their house dusty inside. The neighbor on the other side is afraid that our grading might result in some dirt clods rolling down the hill onto their empty lot. So they want us to buy them an insurance policy indemnifying them from any liability due to earth slippage.*

Some neighbors object to nearly every project their neighbors embark on because they feel that these projects infringe on their privacy, or their parking, or their way of life. Or in the case of one Annapolis, Maryland, homeowner, all of these things.

Dennis and Louise Olson wanted to put a bay window in their kitchen, which would make it much sunnier and improve their view of the cityscape from great to terrific. Because the Olsons lived in a historic neighborhood, they needed permission from the historic commission, which was granted, and from the zoning board. Claude and Margaret Greet lived about fifty yards away from the Olsons, down a hill and three houses to the side. The Greets protested vigorously about this window because they insisted that it would diminish their privacy. (Never mind that the Olsons could have just bought a telescope, or the Greets could have used curtains.) The Greets fought and screamed and acted like little children to keep their neighbors from putting in a bigger window. In the end they lost, but in the process they had alienated many of their neighbors (who sided with the Olsons).

•

Several years later other neighbors wanted to build some steps behind their house into a public alley, which was more like a dirt path. The Greets, whose house also bordered on the alley, parked their car in the alley behind their house, partly on their own property, partly on public property. The Greets happened to be fanatical about their parking privileges because they had out-of-state plates (it's cheaper), and protected their parking place with as much vigor as they protected their imagined privacy. When their neighbor had the steps put in, Margaret Greet intimidated the neighbor's contractor into taking out the bottom two steps, because they interfered with her ability to drive in the alley. (They really didn't.) A classic example of how to be a bad neighbor.

If you are building and it's your right to build, you should still listen to your neighbor's thoughts. But if you know your neighbor to be a stodgy obstructionist and you have all your permits, just build anyway. There's no way to instill reason in somebody like that.

(About a year later, the Greets illegally graveled the grass-covered alley. All their neighbors signed a letter asking them to remove the gravel, because everyone else appreciated having a green strip behind their house. The Greets didn't remove the gravel; instead they made sure that their car was tucked in every night on their property, no longer parked halfway on public land, so that their neighbors couldn't have them ticketed, something they had no intention of doing. One final note: At last report, the Greets regularly call city inspectors to complain about their neighbors. For example, they reported a neighbor they mistakenly thought was illegally draining a swimming pool into the alley. Obstructionist neighbors are like that.)

• • • • • • • • • • • • • • • • • • • • • • • • • • • • • • • • • • • • • • • • •

## BUILDING IT YOUR WAY

Remember what your renovating neighbors did to make you mad; do the opposite.

• • • • • • • • • • • • • • • • • • • • • • • • • • • • • • • • • • • • • • • • •

# 4

# Foliage Wars

You love cultivated roses, a weedless green lawn, a perennial border. She loves wildlife, a wild area, weeds. Normally that shouldn't be a problem, except that she's your neighbor. Honeysuckle creeps over the boundary from her side and strangles your prize roses. Her beloved wild area attracts pests that undermine your green grass. Weed seeds blow over and threaten to choke out your cultivated flowers.

Flowers and trees make for plenty of neighbor problems. Who's responsible for the large diseased trees with branches that threaten to smash your bedroom window while you sleep? Can you believe that guy who grows corn in his front yard? Who's going to clean up all those mulberries? Will you survive ragweed season with your neighbor's bumper crop thriving just a few feet away? What about the black walnut that's poisoning your flowers with its roots?

Basically, the problem here is emotional attachment. Your neighbor has a wild yard because it will save the wildlife, grows corn because her parents did, and planted that tree when her son was born. Your neighbors will be no more understanding of your pink flamingo than you are of their dead tree, which is home to some noisy woodpeckers.

It's best to approach a problem like this with a sense of humor as well as one of compromise.

## No Gardens of Eden Here

Build a beautiful garden and you think your neighbors will appreciate it. Not so, as one Minnesota resident discovered.

*I am a Texan who has had the (mis?)fortune to find a job in Minnesota. This means every year I inevitably try to start my garden too early and I inevitably end up planting it several times. I had only planted it three times last summer when I left (May 24, approximately one week after the last frost date) for a six-week bike tour of Europe. With my luck it froze in June. When I returned some four to five weeks later I discovered a note from the local (small-town) police informing me that I must tend my yard immediately or the "city" would have someone out to do it for me.*

*I was somewhat mystified, because we had hired a young man to mow our rather large yard (50 x 300 feet) and the grass was mown and looking good.*

*It seems they were upset at my backyard garden, which they could only have heard about from our next-door neighbors. (It cannot be seen from the street at all.)*

*The note went on to explain that there is an ordinance in Cold Spring (my booming Minnesotan metropolis) that states a weed may not be taller than six inches; and that several woodchucks had taken up residence on the property.*

*Well, I spent the next week or so weeding out my six-foot-tall garden of weeds and nary a woodchuck did I see. (My setter/lab didn't find any signs of one either.) I can only assume that my beloved neighbors reported me to the police and invented a woodchuck story to validate their grounds for unhappiness.*

*I loved the comment that "several woodchucks had taken up residence on the property" and it still makes me laugh to think about how serious this crime can be! These same neighbors (schooled in the Minnesota tradition of planting a summer vegetable garden and always in neat little rows) always come out when they see me gardening and ask me what I am planting. I have a huge herb garden and a large flower garden and I usually answer, "a few daisies and a few chrysanthemums, a few nasturtiums" at which point the elderly woman always looks crestfallen and sighs in great disappointment, "Oh, flowers." (It happens four or five times the first part of the planting season.) It seems that it is incomprehensible to her that I'm not planting useful plants that you can eat. They also seem very unhappy that my flowers are not planted in rows (like their one row in front of the vegetables—marigolds—probably against the nematodes).*

*I guess I'll never really be popular in Minnesota.*

Some people don't like vegetable gardens at all, preferring lawns—a common conflict. This may be particularly true about new neighbors who have unrealistic expectations about a neighborhood. Here's one such real-life story:

*A few years ago, we lived in "family housing" at a university. The houses were large apartments stacked two high. When we moved in, our downstairs neighbors had a beautiful wild organic garden directly behind our building. They offered to share the space, which we did until they moved, whereupon they left the garden in our care.*

*The new neighbors showed up and we were friendly and neighborly and offered to share the garden with them. They were cool and tentative. Soon we were told by the family housing administration that the garden was being taken out, and the space was being turned over to the new neighbors. Inquiries revealed that the neighbors had lobbied hard to claim the space as their private backyard since "it was in back of their house and under their windows." And after our neighborly generosity! We were infuriated.*

*We talked to the neighbors. "We just want some privacy," they said. "We are going to put in a nice green lawn. It would be so much better to look at than all those weeds out there. We just want a space that's ours." I guess they never learned to share. A lawn?! They were adding insult to injury!*

*We talked to the administration. "Well, it is in back of their* apartment," they said.. "It's in back of **our** apartment too! It's the same building!" we said. "It's been a community garden for six years!" They smiled apologetically and insincerely and said, "Try to understand our position."

We did not. The new neighbors must have greased some palms.

In short, our imperialistic neighbors wrested control of the space and plowed under the garden. The administration made a concession to us and, after much urging, allowed us to form a community garden for all of the family housing residents. There was a great deal of interest and many enthusiastic gardeners. When the space was divvied up, each family got a five-foot by five-foot space.

Meanwhile, the neighbors had watched the community garden grow and changed their minds about the lawn. Now they wanted a garden too. So they planted their huge backyard space in herbs and vegetables and flowers.

While they planted the largest garden in the community, we wondered how we would feed our family of four with our five-by-five garden plot!

As spring came, we started sowing wild birdseed and four o'-clock seeds off the balcony into the backyard. Every day, we went out to "feed the birds," throwing handfuls of weed seed into their newly planted garden. Within weeks the yard was green. Within a month the weeds had overtaken the garden plants and overwhelmed the frustrated gardeners. Eventually, the wild plants took back the garden and choked out the vegetables and flowers and herbs. The neighbors abandoned the garden and let it go to seed.

It remains a wild space to this day.

Garden wars can become downright nasty. Here's one story about two neighbors who disagreed on the philosophy of yards, and how the more yard-wise neighbor won the war (without ever firing a shot.)

Most of my neighbors are nice, but one pair is a pain. They criticize my veggie garden and tell me my "wild" area (used to provide food and shelter to beneficial insects as well as a place to overwinter) looks like the south Bronx. Why is it I can never come up with a quick response at the time? I should have said "Thank you, but I think it needs some old tires" and then opened my garage and thrown an old

*tire into the yard. Oh well. But to get even with them, I made them a
present of a Japanese beetle trap. I was pleased the first neighbor put
up the trap near their roses. I put up an old trap myself but without the
lure.*

*So all the Japanese beetles are lured from my garden into theirs.
When my neighbor told me about the damage the beetles were doing
to their roses, my reply was "Good thing I gave you the trap; think how
bad it would be without it!"*

As I've said on a number of occasions, there are many exam-
ples of what people have done to each other that *I don't recommend
and I don't condone.* But I am including these stories in *Outwitting
the Neighbors* because they are funny, and good as negative exam-
ples. But most of all, these stories reveal how awful people can be
toward each other and why it's crucial to try to understand your
neighbor's point of view. Always try to be as reasonable as circumstances allow. And be ready to bend a little.

Fanaticism breeds fanaticism. When you have a neighbor
who's a bit around the bend, he's likely to inspire crazy acts on your
part. Many otherwise normal people respond to their kooky neighbors by going a bit kooky themselves. This turned out to be the case
in this foliage war:

*I had a neighbor who was a major ecological nut. Everything
had to be good for the environment—chemicals are from hell; we owe
it to our grandchildren; if you can't recycle it, don't use it—that sort
of thing. He was real big on organic fertilization. Every spring and
fall he would dump tons of manure in his yard to get his grass and
flowers to grow, then tell the rest of us how bad we were for not taking
better care of our environment.*

*Three of us got together and decided to help his organic endeav-
ors by going over to his yard at night and pissing on his flower bed.
That pretty much did his flowers in.*

*One night he drove up into his driveway and caught me in the
act. His wife about laughed up her liver but he was not as amused.
When he demanded to know what I was doing I simply told him I was
being "environmentally friendly" and walked off.*

*He never mentioned the environmental issue again.*

•  •  •

•

## A Beautiful Lawn

When it comes to undesirable plants, people often take it upon themselves to get rid of what they don't like in their neighbors' yards. Most of this activity goes on at night. So if you suspect that either a large rabbit or nasty neighbor is rooting your beets and carrots, it may be worth investigating the latter possibility. Here's what one suburban resident found one night.

*My dad thinks dandelions and clover are pretty. His neighbor across the street uses so many chemicals on his yard that he has killed the trees, but the lawn looks great! The neighbor mows his lawn at least three times a week (has to, with all of the chemicals) and usually does everyone else's lawns on the block except my father's. My dad likes the bunnies and other wildlife who live on his property and uses no chemicals at all.*

*The white heads on the dandelions caused a problem last year which began as verbal requests that Dad at least mow his lawn more frequently. One evening, when my father got up in the middle of the night to get a glass of water he noticed a small light in the front yard. He went out to investigate and there was the neighbor with a flashlight and a squirt bottle of RoundUp®, a weed killer.*

*Dad purchased a window fan, which is now positioned facing the neighbor's lawn when the heads are particularly lush.*

What's to be done about your neighbor who refuses to conform to your idea of a beautiful lawn? I'd say a fence is a good start if you can't bend a little.

On the other hand, if your neighbor's idea of an attractive lawn is a totally overgrown weed- and trash-strewn mess, then look into the local laws that might help you.

........................................................................

### Lawn and Garden Appreciation . . . and Wars

If you prefer grass to gardens, attract pest species to your neighbor's garden. Leave pet food outside so garden varmints like raccoons are attracted. Perhaps the gardener will give up.

Share the bounty of your garden generously.

If your neighbor is elderly or disabled, offer to help keep

weeds in the garden down. If you're not inclined to do it yourself, hire a neighborhood kid to do the work.

Pesticides *must* be used according to the labels, or the user is violating federal law. Try reporting your neighbor if you think he's misusing the chemicals.

••••••••••••••••••••••••••••••••••••••••••••••••••••••••••••••••••••••

## TREES AND BUSHES AND DAMAGE CONTROL

Some of the oldest laws on the books stem from tree disputes. Who owns the apples if they fall on your side of the fence? Who controls the border tree? When is your neighbor going to cut down that insect-infested maple? Laws vary slightly from state to state and city to city, but in general neighbors co-own border trees, and one person may not take unilateral action. (There's a lot more on trees coming in the chapter on Property Wars.)

Sometimes the fight just isn't worth it. In Orange, California, a man fighting to protect his shrubs from neighbors who wanted to cut them died of cancer before the court reached its verdict. The man's doctor suggested his disease was caused by the mixture of poisonous oil, gasoline, and charcoal the neighbors allegedly poured over the too-tall bushes. The shrubs were then ordered cut to the exact specifications suggested four years previously before the lawsuit.

When a tree grows on a property line, both neighbors own it. And they must be able to come to some sort of agreement about its care. But a couple of Chicago-area neighbors couldn't come to an agreement about a large elm tree between their yards.

Hope Curtis said the tree roots damaged her brick sidewalk and attracted carpenter ants that spread to her home. She wanted it cut and said it was on her property. Opposing her were her neighbors, John Cuomo and Amanda Connors. They liked the eighty-foot elm.

When they couldn't agree, Curtis took control and called a tree-trimming company. A huge drama followed when the neighbors discovered the tree was about to be axed. They called the police. When the police couldn't mediate the dispute, they called the police chief. The chief called a surveyor to ask him to define the boundary, but he couldn't decide for sure. The tension increased when the tree trimmers climbed the tree to begin work, despite the police chief's

•

order to cease. The chief called the state's attorney who ordered the men out of the tree and threatened to charge them with trespassing. The whole time the police officers were keeping the battling neighbors from one another's throats. The dispute is now being handled by expensive private lawyers.

Open battle is only one result of foliage disputes. Midnight raids are all too common. One woman was surprised to find her new neighbors had taken it upon themselves to prune the boundary forsythias back to nothing. The large bushes that had afforded some amount of privacy were reduced to some stems in the lawn. So the woman confronted the clipper-happy neighbors. But they were unrepentant. Although venting her anger at them gave her some relief, she felt the need to do more, and so she went up to the attic to find the Halloween decorations. She erected a large witch's face in the window facing her neighbors' home. Knowing they look at the malevolent symbol every day has made her feel better about the situation.

She's since moved away from the clipper-happy neighbors. From her story, it sounds as though she could have gone to small claims court to be reimbursed for the cost of the shrubs (but probably not if they regrew). Sometimes it's just not worth the hassle, especially when you know your residence on the block is of limited duration and the damage is minimal. You can just get your satisfaction from making your neighbor look at angry witch faces.

Generally, you can trim your boundary trees and bushes with freedom. But you can't kill them, and if your trimming is done badly, you'll be responsible for the replacement. Also, it's a bad idea to appear one Saturday morning with an electric hedge trimmer and go to work. You should discuss the job with your neighbor first.

If your neighbor is complaining about the walnut tree dropping debris and wishes aloud for a tornado to come along and rip it from the ground, you need to let him know you like it where it is, the way it is. Sometimes neighborly survival skills need to come into play. Perhaps if you volunteer to do a little more to keep your neighbor's workload to a minimum it will make him feel better about the tree. Maybe you can agree to a pruning schedule and share the cost. If you think your neighbor is about to take unilateral action, it's time to put something in writing—calm, diplomatic writing. That way you have some supporting documentation if you end up in any sort of court proceedings.

Although you can trim your neighbor's tree (or he, yours) if the branches or roots are in his yard, it's a good idea to check before you clip. People are attached to their trees and resent it when you hack away at them. Trim only from your side of the property, and don't go in your neighbor's yard unless you have permission. If you kill the tree somehow, your neighbor may sue. The law even protects your neighbor's dead, decaying tree. You may tell him it's dangerous. You can write letters. But until a branch falls on your roof, you can't do much about it. Your insurance probably covers the cost of repairs, but you could probably go to court to recover the deductible. Or your insurance company may want to recover the cost of repair. Then, if you're really mad, you can go to court, taking the letters you wrote for evidence. Take pictures too.

Hire a professional. A tree-trimming company may also take care of any neighbor contact for you. It seems impersonal and un-neighborly though.

In certain circumstances, you may be responsible for keeping your neighbor's trees from damaging your property. Crying after the damage is done may do little good. A Long Islander found this out the hard way. After his neighbor's tree roots did about fifteen hundred dollars' worth of damage to his concrete patio, the plaintiff found an unsympathetic judge. He should have done something when the threat became apparent, ruled the court. This isn't always the case; it is the case that the judicial system can act in unpredictable ways.

In another example, the people on the top of a hill overlooking the ocean wanted to remove vegetation, but the people at the bottom of the hill, fearing landslides, fought the proposal.

The steep hill was populated with alder, oak, cherry, and locust trees that kept the hillside in place, maintained the beach front property owners. The bottom residents suspected the upland dwellers wanted to enhance their view. Still, the city of Normandy Park ruled the top-of-the-hill couple could clear the trees and shrubs if they left the root systems in place and immediately replanted the hillside with fast-growing vegetation.

If tree problems are uprooting your life, it's best to check out your local laws before you do anything. For instance, a lot of communities enacted statutes in the late 1970s to protect solar panels from the shade of neighbors' trees. Many communities have restric-

·

tions on tree height. You may be able to find a law to help you or hinder your neighbor.

Laws that applied when the tree was a sapling apply throughout its life. That's what one Californian found out when he took it upon himself to remove his neighbor's illegal nut tree. A local ordinance outlawed the species. But the neighbor found out the law protected his neighbor's tree since it had been planted well before the law was enacted. He was ordered to pay triple damages. (Many localities have triple damages for wrongly cutting down a tree.) Communities often have laws to protect trees—out of necessity.

In what residents remember as the "Lake Forest Chain Saw Massacre" celebrity Mr. T* chopped down hundreds of trees in front of his Lake Forest estate. The city's new tree protection ordinance forbids chopping down any trees over twelve inches in diameter or standing within thirty feet of the property line.

Mr. T's ax resounded throughout the region, and other communities reacted with similar laws.

Robert Esposito probably used to enjoy pecan pie and chocolate fudge with pecans, but now pecans must leave a bad taste in his mouth. It all started when he asked his neighbors, Skip and Alice Leval, to keep the nuts from their 100-year-old pecan tree cleaned up. Hundred of nuts littered Esposito's drive and yard. The ignored request turned the neighbors' properties in California's San Gabriel Valley into a battle zone.

First, Esposito hired a tree trimming service to come in and cut back the branches. Then the Levals tried to get even by suing Esposito for harassment. Esposito shined outdoor lights in their bedroom window, they said. So Esposito got himself a lawyer and countersued, saying the Levals denied him the enjoyment of his own property. And while both parties were restrained enough to avoid violence, they both had bad aim with a garden hose and soaked one another often.

In the end a judge sorted it all out. Esposito was guilty of spitting at Leval, playing a radio loudly enough to disturb the peace, and squirting Leval with water. His punishment was a fine of $470, two years probation, and ten days' labor on a tree farm.

* Real name.

· · · · · · · · · · · · · · · · · · · · · · · · · · · · · · · · · · · · · · · · · · · · · ·

## TREE TRUCE

Let your neighbor know before you start any tree work on trees close to the boundary.

Share the fruit from your tree neatly in baskets, not strewn all over the ground. That is, keep the mess from your trees cleaned up.

· · · · · · · · · · · · · · · · · · · · · · · · · · · · · · · · · · · · · · · · · · · · · ·

# WHEN YOU CAN'T SEE THE OCEAN FOR THE TREES

Until a constitutional law is passed guaranteeing the right to a view in addition to life, liberty, and the pursuit of happiness, we'll have to rely on local ordinances and other legal devices to protect vistas. You can't simply hire someone to take care of your problem. That's what one Chicago area woman did. She wanted a view of Lake Michigan, so she hired a couple of men to cut down some trees. The problem is, twelve of those trees belonged to her neighbors. And thirty-two belonged to the city. The City of Highland Park filed a lawsuit for $31,000 against the woman.

Thanks in part to citizen Mr. T, the city can file the lawsuit. Just before the woman's action, the city had imposed a law requiring Highland Park residents to seek a seventy-five-dollar permit before firing up a chain saw.

When Rich Moir bought his home on two and a half acres, he looked forward to getting away from neighbor hassles and enjoying the trees and privacy. One June afternoon he looked out his window and discovered the neighbor he had thought was trimming trees on his property had clear-cut the lot next to his, the one that gave him an arboreal view. Now he had a vista of stumps and mud. His neighbor, lured into the lucrative deal because of the high price of timber, was within his rights to cut the wood. Most states don't regulate cutting of small parcels of land. When the federal government limited the timber business on public land, lumber companies turned to private lands for their raw materials.

Sometimes neighbors, angry over another issue, turn on your trees. That's what happened in Laguna Beach, California. Anthony

Bradley, a Washington, D.C., businessman, bought a residence in Laguna Beach because he liked "the casual, relaxed individualistic character of Laguna Beach." Bradley quickly discovered the Californians aren't as casual as he had imagined. Almost immediately he became involved in a property dispute with his neighbors, Steve and Louisa Halperin, over some parcels of land where they were constructing their own dream house.

Soon thereafter, Bradley planted a line of messy carob trees for privacy on his nine-hundred-thousand-dollar estate. The trees grew to twenty-five feet and obstructed the Halperins' view of the ocean, coast, and mountains. In addition, they dropped pods and leaves in their pool and spa. The Halperins quickly decided it was a sort of spite fence and sued Bradley to have the trees removed. A judge ordered Bradley to trim the trees back to restore the Halperins' view of the ocean and mountains.

Perhaps both neighbors now wish they had resolved the problems over cocktails on the deck overlooking the ocean. The same judge also settled the property dispute. He found the Halperins had erected a spite fence of their own, a "monolithic type" wall and ordered them to remove it. He also awarded one parcel of land to the Halperins and allowed them to retain construction footings on another piece of disputed property. At the same time, the judge found Bradley had exceeded height limits on his deck and ordered him to change it or remove it.

In an exclusive gated community in Orange County, neighbors warred over an obstructed view. It appeared that Gretta and Robert Gilbert's new trees would would one day block Steve and Esther Mathers' view of the city and freeway.

Strangely enough, the neighbors had rarely spoken to each other. Said Esther Mathers, "I don't know anybody in the neighborhood." And what's more, she wouldn't know them if she met them at the grocery, she said. So they communicated regularly through lawyers and members of the homeowners association.

When the new landscaping was in place, the Matherses immediately complained to the homeowners association. When the homeowners association found nothing amiss, the Matherses, a retired couple in their seventies, sued the Gilberts in superior court, saying they were harassed by the younger couple. The Gilberts screamed at them, they claim, they shined bright lights in their upstairs windows at night, and Robert Gilbert attempted to run down Edna Mathers.

With enough ill-will to go around, the Matherses are also suing the homeowners association.

A large part of the problem is evident from something Gretta Gilbert said, "A relationship never got established. . . . They never talked to us, never came and knocked on our door."

Here's a case to prove there are many ways to fight. It all started because Barry Pritchard wanted to protect his view. Now he's accused of being a bad neighbor.

Massachusetts apple farmer Richard Shipp feared the apple maggot, the codling moth, and the plum curculio—pests he said his neighbor, Barry Pritchard, harbored in his old apple trees, pests that threatened his livelihood. Pritchard, a lawyer who built his home on land that was once an apple orchard, kept the hundred or so apple trees as a barrier between his home and the road. To Pritchard, the trees provided food and cover for wildlife. To Shipp, the trees represented potential disaster.

So Shipp unearthed an eighty-five-year-old law that permitted agricultural officials to take down abandoned trees presenting a hazard to productive farms. In the entire eighty-five years of its existence, the law hadn't been enforced once until Shipp came along. No matter that there was no evidence of infestation in the trees.

But the plot thickened. It seems that Pritchard had represented Shipp when he bought the piece of land adjacent to Pritchard's property. There was something in it for both men: Shipp wanted to expand his apple orchard, and Pritchard wanted to ensure his privacy by preventing any housing developments from shooting up next to him. Pritchard recalled they had a verbal agreement that Shipp would sell Pritchard some land and sign a deed restriction to prevent a new home from going up next to Pritchard's. And when he approached Shipp to seal the deal after the big land sale, Pritchard said Shipp told him he'd do it only if Pritchard cut down his trees two hundred feet from the property line.

Shipp remembered things differently. It was after Pritchard refused to remove the trees that Shipp decided not to sell the land. A written agreement could have straightened out things here.

Shipp put in a lot of work to improve the land. He tore out the old apple trees, reconditioned the soil, laid new irrigation and drainage pipes, and finally planted new apple trees up to the property line with Pritchard.

·

Shipp saw a threat to his livelihood, something that could destroy his farm. Pritchard saw a threat to his peace, something that could destroy his serenity. Although the court initially agreed with Shipp, they quickly overturned their decision in favor of Pritchard. There is no definitive research that determines when an old stand of trees becomes a threat to other productive, healthy trees. In fact, some old trees harbor beneficial organisms.

The president of the New England Fruit Growers Association, David Robertson, of Stowe, Vermont, perhaps had the best solution to this problem. Since more and more homes are being built next to farms, "We make noise and create smells, which may be disturbing to some neighbors. We have to give a little on this and take a little on that." Probably the best advice of all for getting along.

# 5

# Bad
# Kids

From birth until they move out, neighborhood kids are always going to be a problem for some people in the neighborhood. Maybe the toddler upstairs plays too loudly (Have you ever heard a wheeled walker scoot across uncarpeted hardwood floors? The wood seems to amplify the sound), or the teen across the street has too many friends. Sometimes the problems are a matter of perspective. Sometimes the problems are as real as the graffiti on your garage.

Most problems fall somewhere between the grouchy, chronic complainer and the incorrigible juvenile delinquent. If you can keep your head about you, perhaps you can come to some sort of agreement about the proper solution.

. . .

# WHEN IT'S YOUR DARLINGS

If the problem kids are your own, your perception of the problem is going to be a little different than if someone else's kids are giving you problems. Your little darling needs to practice her tap-dancing if she's ever going to make it on Broadway. What's the problem with the folks in the downstairs apartment? Your neighbors saw your daughter smoking and hanging out with hoodlums? They're just nosy.

You want your kids to have every experience, to develop any skill to the best of their ability, to create, to have tons of friends, and to develop independence and good judgment. Your neighbors want your kids to be homebound loners who watch TV with the volume on low and check with you (quietly) before they make any move. It seems there's lots of room for compromise, unless your neighbors are like these, reported by a woman on the East Coast; they've never heard of give-and-take:

*Across the street lived two next-door neighbors. John had lived in his home about fifteen years, Mark about seven years. John's fifteen-year-old son Tim liked to shoot hoops with his buddies after school. Unfortunately, the hoop was at the end of the driveway, close to Mark's house. Occasionally the ball would go over the fence and the kids would hop the fence to retrieve it (if Mark didn't snatch it first). After a ball-snatching incident John went over to try to reason with Mark and get the ball back. They had "words" and later that night, as I came home from work, I saw Mark's house lit up like an airport landing strip. Mark had bought spotlights and positioned them around his yard pointing at his own house. He had also made signs reading: "Keep Out," "Balls Will Not Be Returned," and "No Kids" (he had two of his own). He put chicken wire on the fence between the houses so no one could climb the fence anymore.*

*I was slightly amused until after about three weeks went by and the traffic on my street increased greatly so that town residents could see the "nut's" house lit up at night. Then Mark came around asking neighbors to sign a petition against John and Tim and the friends to keep them out of his yard. I declined to sign it. It was finally settled when Mark and his wife split up and moved away. The street is finally back to being quiet. John has since passed away, but after Mark moved we would chuckle about the size of his electric bill.*

• • •

Neighbors like this have little sense of humor; they're 100 percent adults with no child left inside them. (Ordinary folks are 75 percent adult, and 25 percent child; real fun adults are 50-50.) There's nothing you can do to change a neighbor like Mark. Assume that he has no outlet for his steam but to vent it on your kid. Look for ways to keep your kid away from him. When neighbors exhibit this sort of weirdness, you never know how things will escalate. One day your neighbor is Ward Cleaver, the next he's Charles Manson.

Although it will be an incredible hassle, remove your child from the conflict until things quiet down. Bribe your kids. Send them to the mall, movies, ski camp. Now is not the time to discuss scheduled hours for play or moving the hoop. It's time to lie low. As a matter of fact, if my neighbor reacted like this one, I might even take my family on an extended vacation.

But some neighbors are chronic complainers. Your kid is jumping rope when they want to nap and the skipping and singing is keeping them awake. Or they don't like the homemade decorations in the window. Some neighbors, frustrated at not being able to complain about your kids, will complain to you about other neighbors' kids.

*As a military wife I've lived in what is called stairwell housing, meaning big apartment buildings that share a common hallway or entrance. That can be very interesting at times.*

*My husband, two-year-old child, and I lived on the third floor. A woman named Tracy who lived on the first floor used to call me up on the security phone and ask me to make my kid stop running over the floor. I would tell her that it was not Rebecca, because she was asleep. Tracy would not believe me. I figured it was the lady below me, as she had a small child too. Well, this went on and on nightly; finally I asked her to come up and see that my child was asleep. She did.*

*After that she would call and complain about the people above me whom I never heard. She even complained about the people above her having sex: said she could hear the headboard pounding against the wall. Once she even asked my husband to put his shoes on in his car instead of walking down the stairs with his combat boots on.*

You don't want to blow your top with people like these. They'll be after your children and you too. The best option is to be calm and firmly refuse to get involved in discussions about problems with other neighbors. Change the subject, and soon the neighbor will be bothering someone else with gossip.

Sometimes, though, a neighbor might have something valuable to offer. Once, being caught in a wrongdoing by your neighbor was the same as being caught by your parents. In fact, you got in trouble twice.

*I didn't know my neighbor very well because we all pretty much keep to ourselves around here. My wife and I both work, and with carpooling and after-school activities and all, we probably didn't see the kids all that much. So they got in trouble now and again. One day the next-door neighbor comes knocking on the door, kind of embarrassed-like. He finally got around to his point, that he saw my daughter dropping water balloons onto cars from the highway overpass. At first, I was really ticked off because my child was none of his business. But then I thought about how dangerous it could be if Becky had been doing something like that, so I asked her. She said she hadn't been doing anything, but I could tell she was lying. I grounded her. Then I went and apologized to the neighbor and told him to let me know any time he saw her doing something like that. He's been back, but not to snitch. Just to talk.*

So if your neighbor tells you he saw your kid crossing a forbidden busy street or teasing a neighborhood dog, listen carefully. Thank your neighbor for his interest and tell him you'll take care of things. Then bring up the issue with your child. He'll probably deny things, but he'll get the message: many people are watching out for him.

• • • • • • • • • • • • • • • • • • • • • • • • • • • • • • • • • • • • • • • • • • •

## PROTECTING YOUR PRECIOUS ONES

Make sure your neighbors know your kids; share fun times with them. Have your kids do little favors such as bring the newspaper to their doorstep, rake some leaves, shovel the walk, or just visit.

Take neighbor complaints seriously. Make sure your kids obey the rules and respect the property of others.

• • • • • • • • • • • • • • • • • • • • • • • • • • • • • • • • • • • • • • • • • • •

## SMALL ONES

Who would complain about an innocent baby? A content toddler? A precious preschooler? What about six of them? When home day care ceases to be an esoteric policy issue and becomes the source of the noise next door, you'll take a stand on its suitability. There's traffic in the morning and evening, a yard full of toys, and most of all, noise.

If the day care provider is doing business illegally, she'll likely go to the ends of the earth to make you happy. And even if the business is perfectly legal, a smart proprietor will want to be a good neighbor too.

Too often people hate confrontation so much that they'll snitch on a neighbor before simply knocking on the door and making a request.

Debbe Montford provides home-based day care for six kids in her Los Angeles area home. Neighbors' complaints about noise and a toy-littered yard prompted her city's planning commission to call a special meeting on family day-care businesses. The business isn't illegal, and Montford considers the complaint an intrusion.

In times of small families, no one is really used to the sounds of six children playing outside. There are some people who don't like to hear a lone toddler trying out new words, so imagine their response to six kids. But many people are also not used to working things out. This neighbor wants absolute silence and immaculate neatness. The three-year-old wants chaos. And with the business of day care comes the traffic of parents dropping off and picking up, the play equipment you have to look at all the time, and the extra garbage overflowing in the back.

If the child-care business is illegal, you can do the obvious and go after the business owner through the official channels. And will your neighbor be steamed! You will have also deprived neighborhood parents of a place to put their kids during the day and will have created a few enemies.

It's generally a smarter idea to pinpoint what's really bothering you about a situation. So in this case, you should consider the noise, mess, or traffic as problems. Then take your concerns to the business owner. Legal or illegal, home day care is a tiring, difficult business, and your neighbor would be wise to deal with you. If you meditate every afternoon between two and four, it's reasonable for your neighbor to keep the kids in then. Living close to other people brings a certain level of security and companionship, and in return you have to give in sometimes. You've got to expect that parents will pick up the kids, but you can expect them not to park in your driveway—or to let their cars idle in front of your house for fifteen minutes.

But if your requests are ignored, you're right to declare war. If the business is illegal, make threats to report it. That should rustle up some cooperation, but if it doesn't, follow through. If the business is legal, consider whether it's violating any other restrictions in the community. Are the kids trespassing on your property? Does the noise level violate any local ordinance (especially between certain hours)? This sort of legal harassment is a shot over the bow of the business owner though, and you can expect countermeasures. The best strategy is soundproofing your house, and fencing your yard. Adjustments like these are cheaper than an ulcer.

It's 2 A.M. and you're awakened by a crying baby. The problem is, the kid's not yours and you can't even see or touch it. It's in the upstairs apartment. The sound of a crying baby is enough to make anyone nuts. And babies cry. At all hours. Sometimes a lot. So if you live in a thin-walled apartment, you sometimes get to experience the worst of parenthood with none of the mitigating smiles, laughs, and funny faces that help parents put up with crying.

What can you do? I assure you, the parents are as disturbed as you are, and they're trying to quiet the baby and get some sleep themselves. But they can't. Complaining and nagging won't do much good. But you can try, like this sleepless guy:

*Every night this kid upstairs starts crying at midnight, just as I'm falling asleep. And his parents let him cry and cry. So one day I have to say something because these people are obviously abusing this kid if he's crying so much. They should stop him because kids shouldn't cry for more than about five minutes. Well, they didn't take my complaint so well, and called me a few names, so I called up the child welfare department. But I only got in more trouble because they told the parents I had made a complaint. Now these people go out of their way to make my life tough. They park in my spot. They drop things on purpose. They buy the kid noisy toys, vacuum at 7 A.M. on Saturdays, and play* Sesame Street *so loud I've learned to count to ten in Spanish. So I'm*

*shopping for a new apartment. This time, I want to be the upstairs*
*neighbor—in an all-adult complex.*

The lament of a single guy. In the end, this neighbor did the right thing; he moved.

If you're lucky, you have this sort of flexibility and can just leave. But maybe you own or you don't want to move. You still have options. Confrontation is tough, because parents are defensive about their kids. Try sleeping in another room. Get a white-noise machine. (More on these machines later.) Try some environmental sound tapes. And test out some earplugs.

(This whole story could have been told from another perspective: "There's a guy in the next door apartment who complains whenever our baby cries. Believe me, we want nothing more than to get Joey to sleep, but complaining doesn't help. He even once reported us to Protective Services because he couldn't stand the crying. This is somebody who's obviously never had a baby—especially a colicky one—and probably hasn't been around children much. A crying baby isn't like a barking dog; you can't teach it to stop.")

The parents may be more open to discussing the crying problem if you can offer some solutions. Perhaps they need carpets or heavy drapes.

The trick is to keep the noise in the kid's room. Offer to split the cost to carpet the kid's room (floors and walls) if you have to. Get some sound-absorbing drapes for the windows. Construct a dropped ceiling of acoustical tile to absorb some sound.

You'll be so busy with these projects that you won't even notice the kid is growing up and not crying so much at night! Then you'd better give some thought to defenses against the next ages of childhood! (These soundproofing techniques work with kids practicing the viola and teens listening to loud music, too.)

••••••••••••••••••••••••••••••••••••••••••••••••••••••••••••••••

## SMALL KIDS, BIG PROBLEMS

Remember that kids will outgrow this stage (and grow into something worse).

Let technology help. The key word is "soundproofing."

••••••••••••••••••••••••••••••••••••••••••••••••••••••••••••••••

•

## KEEPING CHILDREN IN THEIR PLACE

Kids. They go where they want to, they thrive on their secret short-cuts through the neighborhood (the ones in your backyard) and they think decks make cool battle sites (especially yours). And if you yell at them, you're just a grouch and you become a target. So what should you do? Here's one creative solution:

*We had a problem with neighborhood kids cutting through the corner of our backyard. We spoke to the parents, without success. They usually cut through after dark. So I started piling all the dog drop-pings at the corner they went through. After a week, they never did it again.*

This action undoubtedly solved two problems. The one about how to dispose of your dog's droppings and how to deter the kids cutting through the backyard. It's a good one too. Harmless. Effective. Quiet. It doesn't require yelling.

But maybe you don't have a steady supply of poop. Kids are pretty reasonable; it's just that being thoughtful takes too much effort. If their trespassing and playing on your property is just an occasional thing, save your complaining for the days when you really can't take it. Then put on your bathrobe, go outside and ask them nicely to play elsewhere because you're sick with the Black Plague. Cough a lot and tell them how three people at your office have died from it. They'll scatter.

Worse, offer to invite them over to watch some videos you shot of them having diaper changes when they were little. Alternatively, get rid of the attractant in your yard. That may mean cutting down the willow tree they love to swing in or getting rid of the boat (or just garaging it). Without something special, your yard is no more attractive than their own. A high privacy fence works wonders, too. Even if the kids don't normally bother you when they play in your yard, sooner or later they're bound to break something (even if it's just their arms).

Sometimes kids destroy their own stuff, brand-new Christmas gifts or new shoes. Occasionally they manage to mangle their sister's doll. But what happens when a kid destroys a neighbor's possession?

In Sterling, Virginia, Cal Keiler just couldn't forget his neighbor's kids' wrongs, so he filed a complaint. Late at night, long after the nine- and six-year-old perpetrators were asleep, the sheriff knocked on the door.

The kids were charged with destroying a three-hundred-dollar tent after they allegedly damaged it while playing. The tent, according to authorities, had been pitched in a common area near the children's home in Sterling, Virginia. When the neighbor saw several children rolling down a small hill in his tent, he called the sheriff. The children said the wind picked up the tent and blew it while they were examining it. The children became afraid of going to jail and feared their criminal records would keep them from securing jobs when they grew up. Keiler said he only pressed charges because he couldn't get the mother to pay the three hundred dollars in damages to the tent; the mother said he never discussed money with her.

There are parents who abdicate all parental responsibility. "Kids will be kids," they explain as their seven-year-old terrorist swings from a branch of your cherry tree and breaks it off. If you say nothing, you can be sure something similar will happen again. But if you make too big a deal about your precious tree, you'll become the target of much juvenile terrorism and their parents won't take you seriously.

You deserve protection and reimbursement for your losses, but face it, calling the cops on a kid who can't even write his own name is usually unreasonable. If you calmly present the facts to the parents and they don't offer to pay or to repair or replace the damaged item, then you need to be a little more direct. Tell them what you want and the estimated cost. Give them a little time to think about it. The next day ask for half if they won't pay the full amount. Or let the kids work by mowing your lawn to pay their debt. If they won't pay half, they probably won't pay at all, and you've learned an expensive lesson. Don't let kids touch anything you value.

Mary Wolter of Savannah, Georgia, found a way.

*There were two sisters that used to ride across the front yard on their bikes. The parents didn't want to keep them out of my yard. I caught them one day and put their bikes in my garage. When the parents came to cuss me out, I told them they couldn't get the bikes back until the kids fixed my flower beds, which they had ruined. They called the cops, but the bikes were on my property when I took them, so*

•

*the police couldn't do anything. Needless to say, after a week of threats and complaining, I had my flower beds back to normal, and no children walk or ride through my yard anymore.*

Although it's certainly not legal to fight a trespass with a theft, the cop in this situation was evidently some kind of Solomon. The girls were wrong to trespass and damage property. The parents were wrong to fail to discipline their daughters. And the woman was wrong to steal the bikes. Somehow it all turned out right. I don't know how, though, and the results could never be duplicated in a lab. Still, the germ of an idea is to so shock the children that they'll never bother you again. Perhaps you could dress up like a zombie and scare them away. Maybe you could plant your lawn with stinging nettles.

Once you've had a run-in with a kid, though, there's a tendency to want to control him all the time. Try to police the neighborhood kids, and you'll find yourself the target of their tricks. They'll flock to your home at Halloween to soap your windows. They'll plague you with calls about Prince Albert in a can—and worse. They'll go out of their way to cut across your yard. Always count to ten before you react to anything they do in your yard.

Nearly everyone has some sort of memory of a neighbor who was "asking for it," someone who found fault with everything the neighborhood kids did. They were playing in the wrong place, or too loudly, or too violently, or too close to the street. This neighbor was worse than your own parents. And when you got a chance to torment him, you did.

So remember this neighbor when you're dealing with kids in your neighborhood, and choose your battles carefully. One adult cannot rule the neighborhood, and without parental support, you have to be pretty clever.

You teach your kid to listen to and respect adults, and you can expect the same from kids visiting your house. So if your child's playmate breaks the rules on your property, you can send him away and perhaps call his mother. "I'm sorry we have to meet this way, but I thought you'd like to know . . ." Don't be accusatory. Don't lay blame on her kid or her. Present the facts. Be as objective as you can. Say how you feel. If the wrong includes damage to your property, enumerate the damage and what replacement will cost.

Alternatively, you can really stir things up. (Your kid will have to learn to play alone, though.)

*Your brat really screwed up this time. That dumb kid doesn't have the sense not to swing a bat in the house. He broke the TV set. That TV set cost me four hundred dollars, and you better have four hundred dollars in my hands by tomorrow or I'm going to sue.*

The mother hangs up on you, comes to get her kid, and drives on your grass as she backs out of the drive. Things could have gone better:

*"I thought you'd like to know: Alex got a little excited during the Orioles game and swung his bat along with Cal Ripken. He's really upset now because he hit the set and broke it, and he's afraid to come home. I think the set can be repaired."*
*"Oh, I'm so sorry. We'll pay for the repair."*
*"That would be nice. I'll call you as soon as I have an estimate for repair."*
*"Should I come and get him right now?"*
*"Let him stay for dinner as we planned, but why don't you come a little later and have coffee with us?"*

Be prepared for the mother to laugh off the misbehavior, and if she does, realize you won't be getting any support from her. If you continue to call her to complain, you'll only gain a reputation as a chronic complainer. You're not going to get any support on the home front. Send the kid away, take the toy away or scold the child, but never spank or hit someone else's kid. Some parents are even worse than their kids. Just keep away from them.

*A couple of summers ago, we had the ideal candidates for the Neighbors from Hell. Their children were out of control, the husband was a gun fanatic and the wife spied on the neighbors, using her portable phone, among other means. One Saturday morning the children took it upon themselves to throw rocks at our windows. When we confronted them and asked them to stop, the parents threatened us with court action. The father was so enraged that we called the police and considered having a peace bond placed on them. Fortunately, they moved, and their former landlord is now suing them for back rent and damage to the house.*

Sometimes things just work themselves out. An act of God intervenes. Kismet. It happens. Here's one such story:

*Our development is zoned as "horse property"—large lots, stables and barnyard animals allowed. When our house was built the developer created an easement for the properties next door along our back and north sides for access to their stables and to ride their horses down to the riding trails along the river.*

*No problem with that. The easement is fairly well hidden from the house; all the neighbors have to do is ride their horses along it down to the street and then across to the river trails. Fine.*

*The current neighbors, who moved in a couple of years back, had four teenage daughters. The daughters were not too fond of us because every time their boyfriends came over with their boom boxes— rattling windows up and down the street with loud, obscene rap music—the cops would show up ten minutes later and cite them for noise pollution. We weren't the only ones calling. Anyway, the daughters decided to get even with us. When they went riding on the weekend they would gallop their horses across the middle of our lawn, hold the horses in place until they dumped, and generally make a mess in front of our house with their animals. We would complain to mommy and daddy, and the girls would wait until we were both at work and do it again. We caught them more than once churning up our lawn and they would just giggle and smirk at us.*

*We were one step away from filing in small claims court when the problem solved itself. One Saturday I was working on a software program in my study in the front of the house, and I heard horses galloping just out front and excited, happy voices, then an awful crash, a horse screaming, and a girl crying in pain. They had been racing to the stables, cut across our lawn as usual, and where they had to make a sharp left turn to get up on the easement, they cut it too close and ran into our block wall. The wall was built by a professional concrete contractor who used to own the place, and it didn't move. Both girls were thrown; one had a bad concussion and wound up in ICU for a couple of days; and one of the horses was badly hurt. And we weren't in the least bit liable.*

As our insurance company explained to them, (1) the girls knew where the easement was, weren't using it, and so were clearly trespassing, (2) we had previously ordered them not to gallop across our yard, both the girls and their legal guardians, and (3) there was about seven hundred dollars' worth of damage to our wall and would they please send the check as soon as possible?

The girls were grounded for the rest of the summer, the injured horse was sold, and they had to pay the hospital bill themselves, so they were too busy working to see their boyfriends when they came off grounding. Or maybe not: the older two are married and gone now. They never did pay for the wall damage, but we counted that as small loss compared to the luxury of not having a race track in the middle of our yard anymore.

Don't you just love happy endings?

## DAMAGE CONTROL

Keep your head about you when something gets broken and report the damage calmly to the parent. Don't expect reimbursement, but be pleasantly surprised if it comes.

Bellowing like a fishwife at misbehaving kids only attracts more misbehaving kids.

# TEENS

Once upon a time, we were all teenagers. Right?

Loud, rude, obnoxious, kind of ugly when it came to the way we dressed.

Okay, maybe that describes the other teenagers in your neighborhood, but you get the idea. Teenagers are a country unto themselves with their own rules, customs, and songs.

Why even bother trying to change teenagers?

Teenagers are a frequent source of neighbor problems, though not always directly. Sure, loud drumming is annoying, but everybody knows that. What about when your kids don't get along with your neighbor's kids, or with your neighbor (the adult version)? Then problems can really brew. Watch what happened to one such individual:

*Our neighbor has always hated my son, some of which may have been justifiable since my son has always been a bit more aggressive than other boys of his age. I gather that he once went to the man's wife and asked if he could use their pool and, when he was refused, bad-mouthed her (he was nine or ten years old at the time).*

*From that point on, whenever other neighborhood children were invited over, my son was not. Overkill perhaps, but that was our neighbors' choice and helped to teach my son a lesson.*

*It spilled over in other areas, however. One evening someone threw eggs at our neighbor's house. He immediately assumed it was my son and called the police. When they arrived soon afterward, I was able to show them that my son was fast asleep in his bed.*

*A number of us on the street have received phone calls where the caller hangs up. Most of us believe that the calls are a combination of wrong numbers, crank calls, or, most disturbing, thieves casing the area.*

*My neighbor is convinced that my son, now twenty-eight, is the perpetrator.*

*The thing that distresses me so about my relations with my neighbor is that I pride myself on my ability to get along with people and yet I can't get along with him. I'm sure he wouldn't recognize a description of me given by a friend or co-worker or acquaintance or other neighbor.*

Whether you are ultimately successful against unruly teenagers often has a lot to do with whether there is an alliance between the kids and their parents. In many cases, the parents also recognize that their children are a little loud, obnoxious, out-of-control, and a hazard. Under these circumstances, you can forge an alliance between yourself and the children's parents. Think of it as opening a second front. The teenagers are already doing battle with their parents, no doubt, making their lives inside the house miserable. Now you attack, making their lives outside the house less pleasant.

But not always. Some parents are oblivious to their children's actions. When this happens it's up to you to point out the problem, and hope that they see it as a problem.

The worst situations arise when the parents are allies of their teenagers. Hard to believe, but it really happens sometimes. Here's one such instance, admitted to by a former teenager:

*When I was in high school in Nebraska in the sixties, we had some back-door neighbors who were terrible snobs, always comparing their house to ours and apparently teaching even their smallest kids to say "Get off our property" if we happened to walk through there. One summer, toward the Fourth of July, my brothers and I bought a big package of bottle rockets, waited till dark, and then started trying to fire them off in such a way that they'd explode right outside the neighbors' back door. It took about five or six rockets before we got the bottles positioned properly, and then we let loose with a barrage of about ten in a row. Immediately afterward, the phone rang inside our house. My mother, who had been sitting on the porch laughing her head off about the whole thing, went inside and answered. "What? Of course not! My children are inside watching television! How dare you!" It helps that she's been a professional actress all her life. She out-indignationed the neighbors, slammed down the phone, and then just whooped with laughter as we fired off one more barrage of rockets. Then she made us come inside and* really *watch television.*

What can you do when the parent thinks you're a boor and her kids are a riot? Not much, unless you're willing to call the law, which may set you up for more harassment. It's best to ignore taunts for a while to see if things don't settle down a little. Teenagers will lose much less sleep than you will.

If you pursue it, you could end up in court, which is where the Citrons and Reeses found themselves. It all started over a basketball game Bob Reese and his son enjoyed in the evening. Michael Citron and his wife, Diane, said the noise disturbed their peace. Michael Citron allegedly repeatedly sprayed the two male Reeses with a water hose. Reese sued Citron to protect the right of his children to play in their own backyard. Citron struck back with a $2 million suit against the Reeses, claiming injury to his "health, strength and activity." The lawsuits between the men, both attorneys, are pending.

•

# TEEN REC 101

Kids will find something to do and somewhere to be with other kids. If you live near a shopping mall, you probably don't notice teens too much. Like shy forest animals, single teens really prefer that adults not notice them too much. But when they come together, they gain power from one another, and soon the supercharged kids threaten to obliterate everything in their path. Some teens get carried away with their power. And what are the neighbors to do? Go after the parents, for one thing.

As a last resort, some neighbors in Santa Rosa, California, sued the mother unable to control her twin teens, who terrorized the neighborhood with their speeding cars, partying, and noise. They charged emotional damage. Apparently the teens and their friends made five local families prisoners in their homes.

The neighbors won, and now the mother must do something to control her sons. And if they continue to act up, the law will step in again. These neighbors did the sensible thing, they banded together to fight a nuisance. Singly, they couldn't have done it; together, they beat the dragon.

What you can't fight is teen scorn. Teens alienate us with their surly expressions and strange dress; we forget our own past love affairs with similar expressions and dress—and that, inside, we are also secretly children.

Dealing with teens often takes only an awareness that they are, at heart, children and this means taking a firm hand. Is the kid down the street driving you crazy with his littering? Try this approach: "Excuse me, you dropped some trash in my yard. Would you mind throwing it in my trash can at the side of the house?"

Most probably the teen will mumble, "Sorry," comply, and cease the littering. Now he may curse you, but you'll have tried something. And you'll feel better about yourself. It's important to confront, but you have to be careful how you do it.

Teens, caught up in important issues like their hair and new combat boots, are often oblivious to their surroundings. They probably don't even notice you unless you make make yourself obvious. Get a sports car. The trick with teens is to be as nonchalant as they are. Trying to force them to do anything draws attention to yourself and makes your home a target.

In a New England resort town, the teens congregated on the

lawn of the local library, hanging out, eating potato chips, and dropping the bags. The rightly outraged next-door neighbor took her kitchen garbage can over to the teens and lectured them. She commanded them to put their trash in her can. That night, they put a lacrosse ball through her front window.

Definitely the wrong approach. One good way to get results from teens is to divide and conquer. You probably know at least one of the teens in your neighborhood. (He or she mowed your lawn once.) When the others aren't around, take that teen aside and have a private talk. Maybe that teen can influence the rest to party somewhere else.

Most of all, teens like to hang out. What are they doing? "Nothing." How are they? "Bored."

Teenagers want to be with their own friends. Alone. So they end up in parking lots, parks, seashores, and homes when the parents are away. And as a result of their being not quite adults, there's often trouble. Usually it's just noise. Sometimes it's alcohol. Rarely it's violence.

Every town has a problem with teens hanging out. And when they hang out next door to you, it's the worst. Soon they bring their noise, litter, and vandalism. Any attempt to disperse them results in a turf battle. Call the police, and the kids will target you.

Teens may also need just a little organization. Papers are full of stories of what makeovers neighbors have wrought on neighborhoods with a little kid power. Help the kids organize an event or an environmental cleanup—focus that energy in a positive way. Let the kids hang out, and you'll find beer cans on your lawn.

Louisianian Vera Tyson organized her Covington neighborhood to make a beautiful garden out of what had been a local bar. When she looked out her window she saw an empty lot full of trash and weeds. Indigent people started to hang out there, and used syringes appeared with the other trash. Then Tyson and her husband, Barry, and their children, garnered support in the neighborhood to start a garden. They got the teens interested by pointing out they could make extra money by growing and selling vegetables. The mayor went along with her plan and helped out with a lease and provided the liability insurance. They hauled off the garbage, brought in organic material to enrich the soil, and installed a water line. A seed store donated most of the plants and seeds.

•

Make yourself known as an advocate for the kids. When others at a community meeting complain about the hangouts, point out that the kids need to go somewhere, and advocate some sort of supervised hangout. Word gets out, and when Halloween comes around, you won't be on the neighborhood hit list.

Not every teen can be civilized through kindness and reason. Some will drive over your lawn, aim fireworks at your windows, make out in your bushes, leave broken glass on your curb. You have to fight back. With teens like that, complaining to their parents does no good. The parents are glad it's going on in front of your house and not theirs. Some neighborhoods hire private security patrols. If you and your neighbors can afford that, try it. Meet with the police and set up a few siren-screaming raids.

Sometimes neighbors simply can't believe what they see, and they're slow to act. One Californian wanted to share his experience:

*This true story illustrates that there comes a time when something just has to be done. The problem in our townhouse neighborhood (thirty-seven houses arranged in a sort of square around a parking lot) was with preteens congregating at one particular house and then, inexorably, moving into doing more than just congregating. The house in question was home to a family of five. At or about the time when the youngest of the three kids, a hard-looking, brassy-haired girl, reached puberty, the neighbors began to notice that lots of kids (mostly boys, but some girls) had started hanging around the front of their rented house. Presumably some were inside the house, too, but the house was much too small to hold them all, so they sort of "overflowed" onto the front porch and into the very small front yard.*

*This began in March, which was unusually warm that year, and continued with crowds of increasing size over the next month and a half or so. At first it wasn't obvious that anything in particular was going on, but it soon became clear that these kids, ages eleven to thirteen, were drinking lots of beer (and probably using drugs, though we didn't see any).*

*What began as after-school congregating soon degenerated into something to do while skipping school: on some mornings, by 10:30 or so there would be fifteen to thirty adolescents getting drunk. Both parents worked during the day, so the kids were on their own. Rumor had it that the mother was buying them the beer. And, of course, kids of that age don't just get drunk. Soon they were putting the stereo speak-*

ers on the windowsills (pointing outward) and blasting rock music at full volume. Beer cans, and later smashed bottles, were strewn all over the neighborhood.

There were some fights, though not very many. Any neighbors who asked the kids to hold the noise down or contain the litter, and later any neighbors, including stay-at-home moms with small kids in tow, who even happened to pass by, were greeted with a chorus of obscenities and threats. Beer cans were thrown at small kids. As the spring progressed and the weather got warmer, sexual activity became increasingly public and blatant. Several times the police were called, but in this neighborhood the streets are such that the cops could be seen several blocks away as they approached, which gave the kids plenty of time to disperse before the squad car pulled up. This horror would continue from ten or so in the morning until, sometimes, ten or so at night.

The final straw came when a neighbor arrived home after sundown and, trying to back into an empty parking space between two parked cars, almost ran over a boy and girl who were having sex in a parking space. They were too bombed to get belligerent, feel embarrassed, or even retrieve the girl's panties, which were left in the parking space. They did manage to stagger away. I was, at the time, president of the homeowners association, an organization with no police power whatsoever but which many or most people expected to "do something."

So one Sunday afternoon I went knocking on all doors except that one, of course, and invited everyone who was at home to come to an emergency discussion at my house about the problem. About twenty people showed up. All we could think of to do was confront the parents, so we did, then and there. What looked, I'm sure, like a vigilante committee went and knocked on their door, which was answered by the brassy-haired girl. She fled back into the house without a word, and a couple of minutes later the father appeared. We told him that we simply couldn't tolerate the situation any more, and that we'd bring legal action against him and his landlord if it didn't cease. If looks could kill, all twenty of us would have been mass-murdered on the spot. But the situation did cease, and about six weeks later the family moved.

Whew. We didn't flatter ourselves that we'd fixed the problem, since things could have dragged on much longer and gotten much worse. But we did feel very, very lucky.

This story illustrates some important points, defenses that are common to all neighbor problems. First, this man organized his neighbors to take action. Second, the neighbors talked it out with the people making the problem, and while the problem sort of solved itself, the spectacle of the posse probably worked on the parents. And if they had to, the neighbors had already begun to organize to take the next logical step, a formal complaint.

But it also shows a certain depth of curmudgeonliness on the part of the president of this homeowners association—judging by his tone. Still, he managed to get a group of other adults together, and they had the clout to change things.

••••••••••••••••••••••••••••••••••••••••••••••••••••••••••••••••

## TEEN TIPS

Keep your sense of humor about you. Repeat, "They'll grow up and move away" to yourself until you feel better.

Poll your neighbors to see if they're as irked as you. Meet and decide on a solution, whether it be hiring security guards, playing Perry Como albums loudly, or having a meeting with the teen's parents.

Try talking to the offending teenager. It can't hurt.

••••••••••••••••••••••••••••••••••••••••••••••••••••••••••••••••

# 6

# Noisy Neighbors

*I didn't want to kill them, but they wouldn't let
me sleep at night.*
—EDWARD MAZY, A NINETY-THREE-YEAR-OLD
MAN WHO SHOT TWO NEIGHBORS TO DEATH
IN 1991

You think noise is a by-product of modern life? Julius Caesar tried to put a stop to chariot racing on Rome's cobblestone streets because the noise was nerve-racking. So before anyone ever dreamed of a loud muffler, Romans were lying sleepless at night because of a neighbor's thoughtless activities.

Noise comes in all shapes. It's not confined to a neighbor's lawn mower or a teenager's stereo. Just ask the couple in Norfolk, England, who were sentenced to twenty-one days in jail for arguing too loudly in their apartment. After several warnings to the couple and two court appearances, the judge finally gave the neighbors what they wanted. Sentencing the Gabriels, the judge said, "It must be terrifying to live in your block and listen to your shouting and swearing." The Gabriels argued into the wee hours of the morning.

Reported one neighbor, a retired policeman, "They've made life hell for the neighbors. We often heard the sound of breaking china as they hurled objects around. They used every swear word in the English language and got complaints from people living six hundred yards away."

If you've ever been kept awake all night by a howling dog or loud music, no one has to tell you it can cause emotional stress, high blood pressure, memory impairment, and indigestion. Noise tumbled the walls of Jericho. Haven't you thought it would knock down your own at times?

In Britain, five murders a year are attributed to noise.

People have different sensitivities to noise. It's like spicy food: some people can't eat chili that has had a jalapeño waved over it and others eat whole peppers one after another. So are you oversensitive to noise or is your neighbor a lout? Luckily, we have science to help us out in the form of the decibel (dB) scale. Here's how various decibel levels sound and what damage they can do to you. The decibel scale is logarithmic; that is, 60dB is ten times louder than 50dB.

10 dB to 25 dB: Leaves in the breeze, normal noise levels in a bedroom or bucolic park.

30 to 40 dB: Your public library or a living room full of quiet conversation. In a quiet home, the sound level is 38dB.

50 to 65 dB: A group of teens chatting in the McDonald's parking lot; a busy office; normal conversation.

Above 70 dB: These sounds are intrusive; you notice them but may be able to ignore them. A normal conversation in a normal home (with its ambient noise) is about 70dB.

80 dB: You're starting to get annoyed.

85 dB: Sustained noise at this level damages hearing.

90 dB: The noise level of a pig house during feeding time, or standing near traffic at a busy intersection. If you experience 90dB sound every day for forty years, you stand a better than even chance of a 30dB hearing loss. At this level many people think of calling the police.

95 dB: A jackhammer, a ride on a crowded school bus, a power saw, a video arcade, a freight train, a heavy truck, an electric razor (why did you ever think that would be a good gift?)

97 dB: A disco.

100 dB: A poorer-quality jackhammer, lawn mower, leaf blower.

110 dB: a rock concert, a guy in the street yelling at the top of his lungs right next to you.

115dB: a boom box, a car stereo at full volume right next to you.

125 dB: a jet takeoff (nearby)

Above 135 decibels, a person will start to experience physical pain.

140 dB: a military jet takeoff (nearby)

One psychologist said that noise "engenders emotional stress and psychological problems. People troubled by noise are not necessarily more sensitive or neurotic but can become so when subjected to persistent and uncontrollable loud noise. It can also bring on a feeling of despair that can lead to suicide and murder."

Noise affects sleep. Intermittent noise is harder to sleep through than continual noise; noise is worse in the morning, when we are sleeping lightly, than in the middle of the night.

Nearly every community has a noise ordinance, probably banning noises around 80 dB; so if you can measure the noise level, you may be able to get officialdom to come to your rescue. Also, certain noise levels may be prohibited at certain times of day.

But without the uncooperative neighbors who make it, there wouldn't be much noise. They don't care that you can't sleep or concentrate or relax. Conquering noise most often comes down to good neighbor relations or heavy technological investment, like soundproofing your home.

Of all the complaints that people have about their neighbors, noise ranks at the top.

A British man, "driven barmy" by the noise from his neighbor's television, killed him, and was convicted of manslaughter. However, the jury, many of whom evidently had fought off similar impulses, asked the judge to be lenient.

In another British case, apartment dweller Anna Catcher was sentenced to jail for a week for playing music too loudly. The judge said that she had inflicted "psychological torture" and a "nasty campaign of noise" against her neighbors. Catcher loved to play Whitney Houston's hit, "I Will Always Love You" relentlessly at the loudest possible volume. The music was so loud that her neighbors' floor boards shook, and their wardrobes wobbled. But it wasn't just the volume; the same song over and over again started to drive them crazy. Remember, we used rock music to drive former dictator Manuel Noriega from his sanctuary.

Getting pretty worked up over noise isn't just some British aberration. In Elyria, Ohio a man shot his neighbor who was playing his music too loud. A Locust Valley, New York, man stabbed to death his downstairs neighbor after complaining about his loud radio.

So try to work out your problems before a similar solution seems the only possible one to you.

Whether your apartment building or neighborhood is noisy has a lot to do with your neighbors, but it also has to do with the acoustics in your house or apartment. Thin walls and loud neighbors are an exasperating combination. Ultimately (sigh), you may decide that moving is the best path to quiet and tranquillity.

"We can hear everything. We can even hear hangers being hung in the closets. It's a combination of the walls being thin and that we're living next door to the loudest man in the world." That's what one Toronto apartment dweller, Ed Finney, said. "This guy is at full decibel level from the time he wakes up in the morning and whenever he's at home. He's always at full stereo volume. He doesn't seem to talk like a normal person. His normal voice is just loud, fifteen times the volume of the average person." Ed and his wife ended up moving.

Many noisy neighbors work at home. They're carpenters, jigsaw-puzzle makers, drummers, lawn-mower repairmen. I lived for a time next to Steve, a carpenter. He would work in his basement, which was adjacent to our bedroom window, starting at about 6 A.M. When our first daughter was a newborn, his noise wasn't an issue—we were up then anyway. But later we desperately needed our sleep. Steve also parked his truck beneath our bedroom window, so we were often greeted by the sounds of slamming doors.

What could we do? Well, we could have alerted the city—it's illegal to run a carpentry business out of your home in Washington, D.C. But we had a better idea. We talked with Steve, who was able to rearrange his schedule and park his car much further away from our window. He still made some noise sometimes, but we managed to keep good relations with our neighbor and get more sleep.

## LOUD MUSIC, ROWDY PARTIES, SLEEPLESS NIGHTS

You come home from a long day at the office, fix yourself a drink, watch the news. At about eight o'clock, you heat up a frozen meal and eat it while you read the paper. Then you notice a distinct boom-boom noise. Then you remember it's the Friday before Halloween. And a group of students lives next door. By nine the music is cranked up a notch. By ten you can distinctly hear conversations from the party because they've opened the windows. At eleven your glassware is vibrating on the shelves.

A party of this velocity is likely to go on for quite a while, and you'll never make your bird-watching expedition in the morning at this rate. What are your options?

Call the police. You may get no response, but if you do, they could come and quiet things down. This is the only time I recommend calling the cops before a face-to-face confrontation. Face it— a bleary-eyed person in a bathrobe doesn't make the same impression as a cop in full uniform.

Some people just don't like to be told to be quiet. They're a special form of terrorist group.

*When neighbors of a group house of about ten Georgetown University students complained about noise, they wished they hadn't. The students urinated through one complainant's mail slot, dropped a rubber penis through another's, and chased one woman home and dumped garbage in her yard.*

Something similar happened to Janice, a seventy-one-year-old Phoenix resident who was forced to move because of her downstairs neighbor's noise, which she described as "very heavy metal." Janice tried to tolerate the music as long as she could, because she didn't want to seem like a curmudgeon. Eventually she complained to her neighbor, who was apologetic and promised to keep the music down. But he didn't. So Janice complained to the building manager. Then the battle began.

The neighbor played music loudly and often. Janice said, "From that time on, I had absolutely no peace. He began to threaten me. He said he was going to get even. He screamed at me and used terrible, obscene language. I couldn't walk to the mailbox or garbage can without abuse. I had no enemies in the world. There wasn't a person on earth I couldn't talk to—until now."

Stress sent Janice to the hospital. When she returned to her building, her neighbor continued his terror by noise. Janice called the police, but they said that there was nothing they could do about the noise.

One day, Janice's car was damaged in the yard. By whom? She could only suspect. Janice was indeed scared. She said, "He's taken great pains to torment me. Each night when I go to sleep he turns up the stereo louder and louder."

Janice went to court and got a restraining order against the man, but the judge cautioned her that these orders don't always prevent people from doing wrong. Finally, she got the landlord to evict the man.

Even after he left, Janice was still frightened. She did the only thing she could think of to feel safe. She moved to another city.

Human beings can tolerate only so much noise. Consider that a warning to noisemakers. Roger Stewart, a retired mechanic, lived in Yorkshire, England, next to Peter Engle, a disc jockey. Stewart was subjected to relentlessly loud parties that lasted up to seven hours at a time. Finally, after a year of this, he ran into Engle's house while a party was in progress. Stewart threw gasoline all over the furniture, told everyone to leave, and threatened to light a match. The judge who heard Stewart's case described Stewart's "year of hell," and gave him probation, saying, "You have suffered enough." The judge added, "Many decent people might be driven to do the same thing."

Sometimes you'll get no help from others. A cop may scare some college kids, but not hardened, inconsiderate neighbors. And then the cops get tired of trying. Neighbors like these can make your life a noisy hell on earth:

*We have had a variety of neighbors over the years. Just after my husband and I got married, we moved into a trailer park. There were a few permanent neighbors, but most of them were renters who came and went. At one time, we had some obnoxious neighbors who trained pit bull dogs for fighting. We would see them pushing puppies around their kitchen. They would also have loud parties. Mostly men, with just a few slutty women, would get together with a keg or two sitting in the middle of the living room floor. The drunker they got the louder they got. They would leave both doors facing our trailer open and when the men had to urinate, they would simply stand on the steps and pee. My husband worked nights, so I would usually just call the trailer park manager to come do something. I called the cops about the dogs once. We were just outside the city limits, so they said call the county. We called the sheriff and were told to call the animal shelter. They told us that they handled strays and neglected animals mostly and that since the illegal training was going on we needed to call the sheriff. The basic runaround. The neighbors soon disappeared during the middle of the night.*

You can hope your neighbors disappear like these, too. Or you can disappear. In the meantime, get a white noise machine and some earplugs.

If the noise is just an occasional thing, try simply asking for quiet. Here's Stephanie's story. She got quiet, but still had trouble sleeping.

*I was eighteen and newly married, going to college, and I needed to sleep because I had exams the next day at school. My husband and I didn't have much money and lived in a trailer park. It was normally very quiet there, with no problems.*

*One night from about ten o'clock until I couldn't handle it anymore at midnight, I had to listen to a new neighbor's loud music pounding and pounding and pounding; my husband was a wimp (we're divorced now) and would not go over and ask them to turn down the music. So I got up, threw on a robe, and went over. I pounded on the door and then it opened. I just stood there and my mouth fell open as I saw a very nice-looking, muscular man in red underwear, small red underwear . . . silk, looking at me. He had sweat pouring off his body, and it was wintertime in Kansas. He turned down the music and asked me if he could help me and I just kept looking at him. I said to him, "Ah, I've never seen anything like this in my life . . . ." Then I could not believe I had said that and nearly started crying. Then I said, very fast, "Could you play the music lower? I have tests tomorrow. Please?" He said, "Oh sure, I'm sorry . . . I'm lifting weights and sometimes I forget about the time." Well, then he asked me to have a drink with him, and I said, "Uh, uh, uh," and just then I heard my husband calling for me, so I had to go.*

*I didn't get a wink of sleep all night long.*

Often, loud night music is a one-time phenomenon, so you suffer for one night, but not endless ones. In these cases, there's nothing you can do about it. One woman recalled such a night:

*I used to live in a duplex outside Tampa, Florida. Next door lived a mysterious man with a motorcycle. I never saw or heard him for months on end except for a glimpse as he came or went. One night at about three in the morning, his home erupted with earsplitting rock music. As a twenty-year-old student, I had a pretty high tolerance, but this was beyond my endurance. My roommate and I pounded on the walls. On his door. We looked up his phone number and called; no reply. It went on for about an hour and a half, waking everyone in the U-shaped complex. Then the noise suddenly stopped. Then the mystery man resumed his low-profile life, and by the time I saw him to confront him about the noise, it no longer mattered.*

Unfortunately, that's usually what happens. The noise ceases to be relevant when you next see your neighbor. It's hard to fight an occasional nuisance. What are you going to do, call the cops every time the downstairs neighbor turns up the stereo? You all have to agree on some rules, some standards of behavior. And permissible music.

Classical music; rock and roll; heavy metal; jazz; children's songs: these are just a few of the myriad choices we can make when it comes to listening to music. Problems develop when we have to listen to our neighbor's music. Here's one example.

A Seattle man called the police on his neighbor's children because they were playing "It's a Small World" too loudly. But that was the second music complaint. The first complaint had to do with the children's father working on his car in the yard, listening to rock music by musicians with names like Bad S&M and Alice in Chains. His neighbor asked him to turn down the volume. The man refused to turn down the music. The next time the children's father was outside working he was also playing the radio. This time the neighbor didn't fool around. He sent in the cops. When "It's a Small World" started coming in through his windows, the neighbor was sure that it was on purpose. (After all, who would want to play "It's a Small World" at top volume?)

Many noisy neighbors are simply rude about their noise. One

victim, Joanna McCall, was subjected daily to her neighbor's boom box. She put it this way: "The only way to describe it is torture. Often when you complain, they realize they have some power over you, the power to do it again. And then you end up living your life in constant fear of something happening." What's worse is that the music her neighbors were playing was the same Lisa Stansfield album over and over again. Said McCall, "And it's not as if I didn't like Lisa Stansfield's music. I love listening to her, but when I choose to listen to her."

In Albuquerque, New Mexico, the Morrisons had new neighbors, the Davises. The Davises brought with them eight children, which might concern some people, but not the Morrisons, because they had nine kids. But the Davises also had four Rottweilers. These dogs created an air of menace: four Rottweilers are a serious threat. The Davises let their dogs poop in the yard all the time; soon the yard was filled with the worst stench the Morrisons had ever known. But it was the noise that got to the Morrison family: the Davises would yell at each other nearly every moment they were awake. They played heavy metal music until dawn. Dan Morrison complained a few times, but nothing happened. "If you asked the Davises to be quiet, they'd just jeer and clap their hands." Another neighbor suffered a nervous breakdown. That neighbor wrote the Morrison family, "I know what you are going through. Don't let them do to you what they did to me." Still another neighbor left the neighborhood. (The Davises were moved into that house by the city, so they were ensconced. More on the Davis family in the chapter on Weird and Uncivilized Neighbors.)

Sometimes money can solve your noise problems. If your particular problem is the teenager next door, then buy that kid a pair of headphones. Sure, the kid's parents should have taken care of the problem, but that's beside the point: you want the noise stopped. There's nothing like peace and quiet, and fifty dollars isn't too high a price to pay. You'll have to put your ego aside to accomplish this, but the choice is yours. In my opinion, getting what you want is sometimes more important than how you get it.

If the noise that disturbs you is a pretty regular thing, then you can probably fight it. Where visits and pleas from you don't work, and the cops are just as ineffective, the courts may come through. First, find out if the sound violates any noise restriction. Most localities have laws about noise, and it's within your power to measure that noise. You can pick up a decibel meter at some electronic stores and through specialty catalogs. Irreparable damage to the ears begins at about 90 decibels. But you're much better off having an official read the meter—either a police officer who's trained in it, an environmental agency official, or a professional sound consultant. (Take a picture of the meter reading, if no official is available.) Your reading of a decibel meter may be dismissed in court, since you have no expertise in monitoring sound.

Antinoise legislation is hard to enforce, so there needs to be tolerance and common sense. A vacuum cleaner or a blender may be loud enough for a noise restriction, but it's not constant. However, weekly band rehearsal is predictable and probably too loud.

Live music is the worst. Complain and you're an enemy of art. Live with it and you get circles under your eyes.

In St. Cloud, Florida, a young band, appropriately named Mayhem, was driving the neighbors to madness with its rehearsals. In perhaps one of the most creative and satisfying solutions I found in my research, the rock musicians and the neighbors were able to work things out despite some pretty dramatic tactics to stop the noise.

After reading about the dispute that pitted neighbors against the band's lead singer and his parents, the owner of a local sound studio decided to help out. He offered to let the band practice in his soundproof studio for free. As long as the practice didn't interfere with the business in the studio, the band could practice there after hours. Since the studio was able to contain noise of up to 100 decibels, no neighbors would complain.

This was the solution to the problem that thirty-one visits by the sheriff couldn't solve (because he didn't have a noise meter, the sheriff couldn't measure the sound and determine if it exceeded the permitted 60 decibels).

Even though the noise is gone, relations may never be the same in the neighborhood. Disputes over Mayhem's practice schedule led to charges of battery, an angry letter campaign, stolen band equipment, a petition, one heart attack, and threats of a lawsuit. One neighbor borrowed a professional sound system to aim noise toward the home of the sixteen-year-old lead singer and his family.

Fortunately, the problems can sometimes be solved more easily. All it takes is a little communicating.

A professional musician and her neighbor found peace when they agreed on a practice schedule. Then the neighbor knew when to expect noise and could adjust to it. Part of the problem with noise is adjusting to it. If you know there is garbage pickup every Tuesday morning at seven, you're prepared for the noise. If they show up on Thursday, it's annoying. Your senses hate noisy surprises.

Famous neighbors are often noisy neighbors. Famous neighbors give loud parties, they have visitors all day and night, arriving in limousines and sports cars with loud stereos, they have loud arguments with their agents. Of course, if you live next to a famous neighbor you should (1) expect these problems, and (2) have enough money to soundproof your house. But that's not always the case, especially if your neighbor is a musician, for whom noise—that's "music"—is the essence of life.

Smokey Robinson's* neighbors, David and Hallie Inverness, in Encino, California, complained that his loud music playing caused them "humiliation, mental anguish and emotional and physical distress." And if you're going to file a lawsuit on one count, you might as well enjoy a twofer, the Invernesses also sued to have a ten-foot-tall spike hedge removed. For the sake of comparison between the two neighbors, Smokey Robinson's house was valued at $1.5 million; the Invernesses' house at a mere half million dollars. The Invernesses were particularly annoyed by the outdoor yard speakers that they claimed blasted music from 9 A.M. to 10 P.M. at considerable volume. The music caused the Invernesses "great nervous distress."

This isn't the kind of noise you can fight with technology. A tape of ocean sounds will be obliterated by rock. A white noise machine doesn't stand a chance.

In many other circumstances, I've found one of the most effective means of fighting noise is a steady white noise, a hiss or hum that lulls me to sleep. In the summer, the hum of an electric fan is a soporific. In fact, at the president's house at Dartmouth College, electric window fans are the weapon of choice against the noise from fraternity row, where the house sits.

•  •  •

* All names have been changed in this book, except for those of celebrities.

•

## FINDING PEACE

If you live in a neighborhood with a lot of college students, be nice to your beat cops. They'll help keep the peace for you.

Collect an arsenal of noise combating technology: have on hand earplugs, an audio tape of soothing environmental sounds, and a white noise source. Use them all at the same time if you have to.

Amass defensive noise to use against your enemies when there's no hope of a solution.

## CONVERSATIONS

Apartments are especially troublesome. You can hear your neighbors talking, snoring—and worse. Geography and architecture have everything to do with noise. If you are one mile away from your nearest neighbors, chances are that you aren't going to have many problems in the way of noise. If, however, you live on the second floor of a Manhattan apartment building, as I did for eighteen years, then you're going to become aware of noise. Some buildings are built better than others. Witness what happened to this couple from a medium-sized town in Wisconsin:

> When my husband and I were first married, we lived in an ancient apartment over a loan company office in the middle of downtown Appleton, Wisconsin. (The place was so old that it had a built-in icebox, the genuine put-ice-in-it kind, in the kitchen.) Now, the city had ordinances governing how much "light and air" had to be accessible to each bedroom in an apartment, and when the place was first built there was a crawl space into which windows opened from each bedroom in the two apartments occupying the floor. But at some time in the past that crawl space had been roofed over, and that meant windows in each apartment opened out into a black tarpaper space with no light. So the light-and-air requirement had to be filled some other way, and somewhere along the line a very large skylight had been installed. Alas, it was installed right in the center of the building, which meant that it straddled the wall between the two apart-

*ments. It was shaped in such a way as to become a natural mega-*
*phone. This meant that one got to be on very intimate terms with one's*
*neighbors very quickly. While it wasn't a problem when our original*
*neighbors were living in the other apartment (they were close friends*
*of ours) it did become a problem when they moved out and the "Jesus*
*freaks" moved in. Although I think their all-night prayer meetings*
*bothered us more than our newlywed nocturnal activities bothered*
*them, we wound up sleeping on the couch in the living room most*
*nights, since it was hard to convince the landlord that prayers were a*
*bad thing that merited eviction. Eventually the "Jesus freaks" also*
*moved out and the "cavemen" moved in.*

There's also the eye-for-an-eye tactic: be sure to awaken them
in the morning when you leave. If you have nothing to lose, give this
a try. After all, what will they do, keep you awake at night? This isn't
always a practical strategy, because noisy people often are immune
to loud sounds. However, if you attack the problem correctly, things
may work out in your favor. Besides, it makes a great story.

*The lower life forms who inhabited the apartment after the "Je-*
*sus freaks" moved out were the type of people who would drink each*
*other under the table till the bars closed, stagger home, and turn on*
*their four-foot speakers and thump away all night. I think they owned*
*only one album, the Steve Miller Band's "Living in the USA" (to this*
*day I'll break the sound barrier running to change the radio to a dif-*
*ferent station if that song comes on the air). We complained and com-*
*plained and complained to them and to the landlord, but they never*
*could seem to quiet down for long. We called the cops several times,*
*and one night when the marijuana smoke in the hallway was so thick*
*it was hard to see and the neighbors were giving old Steve Miller one*
*more workout, we figured we'd call the cops and get rid of them for*
*good.*
*No luck, alas; the local constabulary merely gave them a ticket*
*for excessive noise, and that was that. So we figured we'd take matters*
*into our own hands. By that time, my husband was working nights (I*
*still had to be at work at 8 A.M.) and he usually got home from work at*
*the radio station at about 6:15 A.M. One morning, he brought home a*
*record that contained a full fifteen minutes of U.S. Marines recruiting*
*ads, plus a couple of John Philip Sousa marches and the National An-*
*them. We made plans. The next morning, when our neighbors had*

•

*fallen into their usual sodden sleep about 5:30, I got up, got dressed for work, and waited for my husband to come home. Then we put that record on my small stereo in the bedroom, turned the speakers to the wall, turned the volume up full, put the turntable\* on repeat and went out for a leisurely breakfast at an all-night restaurant. I left for work right after breakfast and my husband told me he came home to find the record still playing, heel marks on our front door and the neighbors apparently gone for the day. From then on, any time they started making a racket at night all I had to do was stand under the skylight and holler "Join the Marines, fellas!" and they'd quiet right down.*

Of course, during my researches I came across many people who didn't have answers to their neighbor problems. They wanted help, and hoped my book would provide salvation. This plea was typical:

*When can I get a copy of your book? I have a nasty neighbor problem that I need to solve now!! I live in what used to be a quiet peaceful place with only two neighbors. My new neighbor on one side is a young kid who still thinks it's cool to play his music at an ear-splitting level. Not only that but about once a week, usually during the week instead of the weekend, he has to have a few friends over and the ritual is that they all crank up the music loud enough so that I have to turn my own TV up very loud to hear it, then they get drunk and then for some reason they all have to go outside and yell, "WOOOOOOOOOOOOOOO!!!!!" at the top of their lungs! Geez, I'm ready to go crazy.*

*Fortunately, my landlord is his landlord also. I'm thinking of getting my landlord to be the heavy in this one. The problem is, I don't want to make an enemy. I have heard horror stories of people who make enemies of their neighbors, and I just don't think it's worth it.*

The sad part of neighbor relations is that you often can't have both cordial relations with your neighbor and sanity. Which isn't to say you shouldn't try. A civil note worked for one West Hollywood man. When his upstairs neighbor clopped around in heavy shoes at all hours, he just wrote him a note asking him to take off his shoes when he entered the apartment. The neighbor did the neighborly

---

\* Remember turntables and records?

thing, complied, and even wrote back to ask if anything else were wrong.

A woman in Montreal found the only place she could find peace from neighbor noise in her apartment house was by sleeping in the bathtub. The couple on one side had long, loud fights. On the other side was one of those loud talkers. He held court with friends until the wee hours every night. She could even hear his answering machine when he played his messages.

••••••••••••••••••••••••••••••••••••••••••••••••••••••••••••

## FIGHTING BACK

Mention in casual conversation to your problem neighbor something personal you've overheard him discuss. When he acts surprised, tell him you hear everything through the walls.

Your neighbors would be horrified if they knew how their conversations passed through the walls. Suggest noise abatement schemes to help.

••••••••••••••••••••••••••••••••••••••••••••••••••••••••••••

# NOISE YOU'D RATHER NOT HEAR—OR DISCUSS

Sometimes it only takes a word to stop the irritant. In Tulsa, Oklahoma, a family's religious chanting disturbed their neighbors who shared a wall with the chanters in a semidetached home. Many people would find having chanters next door an impossible situation, one with no potential resolution. But in this instance all the neighbors had to do was ask the chanters if they could practice in another part of their house. When the noisy neighbors changed to a different room, they no longer disturbed the folks next door.

Some situations in apartments are too embarrassing to deal with. A woman in Montreal had next-door neighbors who disturbed her with their noise. But she was too embarrassed to discuss it with them. She heard people laughing at odd hours in the night and screams. It happened several times a week. Then she realized her neighbors were making love.

In Arizona, a code enforcement officer answered a complaint about screams and smacking sounds coming from next door. When he knocked on the apartment door, a woman answered the door in her underwear. He quickly realized she was entertaining and enjoyed being spanked while making love.

Or how about the neighbors of a university area who called the police about screams in the night that kept them awake? The screams were coming from a student who was having sex two or three times a night. Eventually she moved, as students will, and peace returned to the neighborhood.


## MACHINERY

A Canadian couple hired a contract killer to take care of a particularly noisy teen. His souped-up car made too much noise.

Sometimes a perception of noise is a matter of opinion. Wind chimes? I love them, but not within earshot of my house. Then I hate them. But not everyone agrees. The issue prompted a letter to Ann Landers and had a Calgary woman in tears when she called a local columnist to complain. Birds singing at the feeder? Again a matter of opinion. A bonging basketball? The sound of children playing happily? Everyone has a different, least favorite, noise.

Most towns have noise ordinances. It's a simple matter of looking up your local laws in the library. Once you've found the law, show a copy to your neighbor. Often when confronted with the written rules, the neighbor will quiet down. Often, but not always, of course. You might try to involve the police, but this can be an unproductive approach. Said one upstate New York police officer: "We just don't have the manpower to go out and try to settle a neighbor dispute—unless there's a fight going on."

Sometimes noise is mechanical and unpredictable, or somewhat so. You can be sure that when leaves fall, the leaf blowers are going to be out in force. Some people have never heard of a rake. But you're not really sure which day or at what time the noise will occur.

If the noise of leaf blowers bothers you—and they're all around—consider changing neighborhoods. Who uses leaf blowers? Mostly gardening services hired by people too busy with their professions to find time to work on their yards. Relatively few homeowners own leaf blowers. Why? Well, they're too noisy.

That's what one Massachusetts woman discovered. When she lived in a rural, well-to-do area, she found she and her two young children were about the only people in the neighborhood during the day. She never saw her neighbors, who had a six-foot-plus wall to shield them. Still she felt pretty sure people were alive on the other side of the wall, because every year, fall and spring, a contractor came with giant vacuum-cleaning trucks and did something to the yard—who knows what?—it was impossible to see over the wall. As you might have guessed, the workers arrived at naptime.

If you suspect a noise is actually harmful, measure the sound. Talk with the workers first. While most contractors pursue the easiest course and would prefer not to do anything to quiet their machinery, if they realize that you are serious about doing what needs to be done to attain quiet, they may be reasonable. Nobody likes to be fined by the city. Often workers can take physical steps to quiet or muffle machinery.

Ultimately, only a lawsuit may bring peace and quiet back to your home. But lawsuits don't always succeed, and if you are considering suing your neighbor (a tactic destined to sour relations forever), keep in mind several points.

First, if the noise was there before you moved into the neighborhood, and you knew about it, then your chances of winning a lawsuit are diminished. For example, let's say you were aware of the little drummer boy—a seventeen-year-old kid who played loud and late from time to time—before you moved into the neighborhood. Months after you moved in you started complaining, and your complaints led nowhere. So you sued. Because you moved into your house fully aware of the nuisance, you may have lost some legal ground. Still, you could argue that you thought the kid would go away to college; there was no way for you to conceive that he would be starting a rock and roll band instead of getting an education. It's these finer points that are for juries, lawyers, and judges to argue.

## NOT EVERY NOISE IS REAL

Jonathan Blair banged his broom handle on his ceiling every time he heard people walking in the apartment above. He also yelled from his window at his neighbors when they were walking in the street, telling them to be quiet. Blair called the police every time his neighbors gave a party—trouble was, there never was a party when he called. He badgered and terrified a couple in a nearby apartment so that they would only watch television with the sound off.

•

Ham radio operators are frequently subjected to the mystery noise complaint. (Only the noise comes in over the TV, telephone, radio, or bridgework.) If there's a strange-looking antenna on your roof, somebody's going to complain. Here's what happened to one amateur radio operator:

*My neighbor insisted that I was getting into his telephones, causing them not to be able to place or receive calls. He said he could hear me talking plain as day, and even quoted part of a conversation I had on the twenty-meter band, talking about our going to a Florida Marlins game in Miami one weekend.*

*I spent many hours trying to track down the problem, and I finally installed several K-Com filters because I thought they'd solve the problem (although I personally had never experienced it in action).*

*The problem turned out to be someone with a cordless (old 49 MHz job) on the same channel as my neighbor's ancient GE cordless. Since we live in an area with a large percentage of part-time residents, it was a long time before the owner of the mystery telephone showed up and used his phone. But as soon as he did, the problem returned. Fortunately, I was out of town at the time, proving once and for all that it wasn't my fault!*

*Moral of the story (and I should know it well by now): Don't try to fix something until you know what the hell you're trying to fix!*

A British citizen complained that his neighbor's parakeet was too noisy. When the parakeet owner didn't do anything to resolve the problem (what can you do, teach the parakeet to say "Shh"?), this sound-sensitive individual told the neighbor's son that his mother was a prostitute. Previously he had reported the woman to the RSPCA. When that didn't produce results, he dumped grass clippings in her yard and started to photograph her hanging laundry to dry.

Ignore crazy neighbors who are so sensitive to sound that they hear phantom noise. If you can. Other complaints you should take seriously. People have varying tolerances to noise, and we have to respect that. While you may think you're watching television at a reasonable volume—and you no doubt are—see what you can do to stifle your neighbor's complaints. Neighbors annoyed by noise can be troublesomely unrelenting.

# 7

# Horrible
# Pets

There's a famous story that goes like this:

A woman called her neighbor at 4 A.M. to complain about his dog barking. The man thanked her, then hung up the phone. The next morning at four o'clock he called the woman back. "Madam, I have no dog," he said.

Dogs are wonderful. As long as they belong to *you*.

Cats, too, are cute. But as with dogs, if every neighbor liked cats, then all your neighborhood would be in heat the year around.

Disputes between neighbors over pets erupt frequently. Often they end up in court, especially if somebody is bitten or knocked down by a dog. But even the court cases don't go smoothly, as in this lawsuit. In San Antonio, Texas, someone complained that the barking done by another neighbor's two dogs caused "psychological pain." The barked-at neighbor had sprayed Halt at the dogs to get them to stop barking. In court, the plaintiff's attorney asked his client about spraying Halt, a pepper-based chemical dog repellent. "Like this?" the lawyer asked, and he tapped the spray button. The spray went all over the jury.

Mayhem. The jury scattered all over the courtroom, like, well, like dogs sprayed with Halt. The judge temporarily halted the trial.

Roaming dogs cause trouble. As do their feline counterparts. And goats, chickens, and pigs, not to mention stray cows, horses, and hawks.

## BARKING AND CLUCKING AND HOWLING AND . . . WHAT WAS THAT?

A dog barks in the night. And barks. And people lie awake and think of . . . guns. In Irvine, California, a neighbor followed through and killed a dog that kept him awake by barking.

In Ojai, California, the problem was a little more exotic: birds. Not just little sparrows at a feeder. Major birds. Parrots. Loud birds.

Bird breeder Kay Nesbit's aviary, the Bird in the Hand Exotic Bird Farm, had neighbors squawking. Nesbit kept over one hundred parrots, cockatoos, macaws, and other exotic birds.

She said she was doing good work, breeding birds, some of them listed by the federal government as endangered species, and shipping them across the United States. Without her birds, she said, people would be buying birds caught in the wild, a practice that further depletes the population. So she had many supporters, but none of them were among her neighbors, who complained about the screeching and squawking. Neighbors said the sounds invaded their homes. Nesbit said the neighbors were hearing peacocks on other property and birds attracted to her home because of the parrots.

The fight went on for years. There were petition drives, public testimony, a slander suit filed by Nesbit, and then county-ordered sound modifications

Nesbit didn't understand why neighbors complained. She lived in a rural area zoned for agricultural uses. Schoolchildren visited to learn about ecology, and she took her birds to visit facilities for the handicapped. To date, Nesbit has built a five-thousand-dollar sound barrier, but her neighbors claim they can't hear the difference. Neighbors separated from Nesbit by as much as five acres still find the noise annoying. Measures of the sound found the noise was within acceptable county guidelines. To Nesbit's psychic benefit, her closest neighbor supported her. At a hearing, the neighbor said she found the sounds to be "natural" if sometimes "quite loud."

In another animal case, police surprised riders from Glenview Farms with summonses after neighbors complained about the noisy horses. The farm, located in Long Island's Laurel Hollow, is a well-known stable of the riding set. It seems the horses violated a 6 P.M. to 8 A.M. noise restriction in the village. Glenview Farms, where they also gave riding instruction, came under censure as well. The clip-clop of horses and the riding instructors' commands bothered some neighbors. The police came but didn't arrest anyone.

Animals are part flesh, but mostly vocal cords. In fact, an animal behaviorist clocked a cocker spaniel that barked 907 times in a ten-minute period. Plenty of homeowners associations recognize the problems dogs can cause and have rules against dogs' barking or whining for long periods of time.

There are antibark collars which deliver a shock to the dog when he barks or sound-activated sprinkler systems that soak noisy dogs. But dog trainers pretty much accept that it's pretty near impossible to train a grown dog never to bark. The trick is to remove the stimulus.

Sometimes medication—oops, that's mediation—can help solve the problem with barking. Mediation with the dog's owner, not the dog. A Toronto resident, irritated by barking dogs in the middle of the night, turned first to the police. When that didn't help, he went to a mediator who helped the victim work out a deal with the dog's owner. Simply moving the dogs away from the distractions that stimulated them to bark made for a night's peaceful sleep.

Keep a record of the barking dog problem. Gloria Jean Wiseman of Los Angeles made tape recordings and kept a written log of barking problems and then went to a city animal control hearing. The tapes weighed in her favor.

Sometimes the hearings don't produce the results wanted. The stakes are high. Because the dog may be ordered out of its home (in other words, destroyed) the hearing examiners take great care in making their decisions. Another Angeleno was accused of splicing audio tapes to exaggerate the barking problem. Another hearing ruled in favor of the dogs, because the man couldn't prove which dogs were barking. Like any court system, the animal control courts are slow and backed up with cases. You may wait up to a year for a ruling with appeals and such.

That's what San Francisco's Jean Dunn found. She fought the noise from the dog next door for a year and a half. In the end, her problem was solved by constructing a walkway that contained the dog away from her property line—and her bedroom. But the solution was hard won, and her neighbor fought her at every step. When the court ruled the dog be fitted with an electronic collar that shocked it when it barked, the owners accused Dunn of inciting the dog to bark.

Violence against dogs is unusual, but it happens. It's an unconscionable deed, and when you think for a second about it, the dog can't help barking. It's the owners who are irresponsible (not that I advocate harming them either). But barking dogs sometimes cause neighbors to come to blows. A California woman who had suffered barking for two years snapped one day and shouted at the dog's owner. The dog's owner's sister attacked her and hit her with a pailful of water mixed with dog feces. The pail cut her, and the wound required ten stitches. A judge found in the woman's favor and ordered the dog owner to pay $1,500 in damages.

The next method worked, I guess, but we're lucky the dog didn't die. When a dog is harmed by a neighbor, the dog's owner should share some of the blame. Sadly, the dog is often the focus of the solution, much to its misfortune.

This story illustrates the point that it's not the dog's fault—people are to blame when it comes to barking. If there's a loud dog, an inconsiderate dog owner, and a nasty neighbor, here's what might happen:

*At the present time we live in an apartment building with six two-story townhouses over a row of individual garages. Two years ago, we had living next door to us two twenty-somethings with a collective IQ of about 75 and the social skills of a caveman with a toothache. As if their incessant heavy-metal music thumping through the wall wasn't bad enough, they also owned a little Pomeranian that was not housebroken and was not bark-broken either. So when the boneheads went out, they used to leave the dog downstairs in the garage, where it would yap its little head off continuously till they got back. One day my brother (a construction worker) and three of his friends were visiting. He got annoyed at the yapping from downstairs, went to check, and found out that the boneheads had forgotten to lock the garage door. So my brother got an old blanket and a big roll of gaffers tape out of the back of his truck and he and his friends went down, cornered the dog, threw the blanket over it to catch it, and then taped it firmly to the floor with the gaffers tape. We decided right about then that it would be a good thing if none of us were around when the boneheads came home, so we all left. They had to cut a lot of the dog's fur off to get it loose from the tape, which made it look about as bad as it sounded. We like to think that maybe that helped them make the decision to move out a month later.*

If barking bothers you enough, you can go crazy, at least a little. Through this story, I'm merely reporting the magnitude of rage that's trapped inside many people, waiting to explode. A better solution, naturally, would have been to tape the boneheads to the floor. But they might bite. The solution in the next story is a little more innovative, but it also shows the depth to which people will go to silence the wild barker in their neighborhood.

*About six months ago a young woman moved into the apartment next door, with two dogs who like to serenade the neighborhood continuously while their owner is away. And she's away a lot.*

*We tried everything to get them to stop, from kicking the wall to getting a dog whistle. Nothing worked. The owner even tried muzzling the dogs, and that didn't work either. What finally did the trick was having my son, who is six feet five and in top physical condition, lean off the balcony and whip a small water balloon into the middle of the sliding glass door on the balcony next door. The explosion invariably produced a yipe from the dogs and then blessed silence. I don't know what the neighbor did with all the water and lacerated rubber on her balcony, though.*

Dogs bark. It's only their nature. And it's our nature to get irritated by it. Dogs bark when they're lonely. When they're bored. When they're excited. When there's a fire engine that's racing by off-key. And when they're angry. But not when they sleep, so you're guaranteed a couple of hours of silence now and then.

Puppies can be trained by their owners not to bark, but not by frustrated neighbors. The dogs simply don't care what *you* think. They serve their masters. If you can get the owner to agree with you and train the dog, maybe you'll have some peace. Offer to pay for dog obedience training. If the barking is driving you crazy, that's probably the only way to deal with the problem and still be friends (or at least not enemies) with your neighbors. If a barking dog is bothering you, in all likelihood your neighbor is aware that his dog is a bit loud, so your offer to have the dog trained might be appreciated. Try it. It sure beats dog court.

.........................................................................

## THE QUIET PITTER-PATTER OF PETS

Try to find out what's making the dogs excited enough to bark. Eliminate the stimulus. Ditto with chattering birds.

Keep records—a logbook—of the bothersome noise. Make recordings if you must. Then present your evidence to the animal's owner. Threaten to go to court if the owner won't cooperate.

Slip the phone numbers for several animal trainers under your neighbor's door. Offer to pay for any training.

Seek allies in your neighborhood. Who will those allies be? Most likely anybody *and everybody* who doesn't have a dog. And those who have quiet, well-trained pets.

.........................................................................

## THEIR "CALLING CARDS," WHICH IS A NICE WAY OF SAYING . . .

You find it on your shoes. Smeared on your carpets. Around your roses. You complain. The pet owners say, "Hey, he has to use the bathroom somewhere!" But not in your yard. What should be done? Diaper the dog? Sure, he has to go somewhere, but preferably where his master is right behind him with a pooper-scooper.

But if you can't get the master to walk the dog and clean up after it, one option is to make an impenetrable fortress of your yard, as one upstate New York family did:

> *We moved into a tiny house in a 1930s subdivision at what had been the outer edges of Albany in the 1970s. Our house had only a wee, shaded backyard, but a nice, large, sunny front yard for the size of the normal plots. I decided to turn my front yard into a garden.*
>
> *At first, we dug a few flower beds around the perimeter. The impact of the neighborhood dogs, who were supposed to be tethered, was awful. They dug and deposited.*
>
> *In response, I decided to put up a nice, low (lower than city regulations for maximum height of a front-yard fence) white picket fence. When it went up, there was a hue and cry from all the older residents that I was ruining the neighborhood.*

Unfortunately, this resident eliminated one neighbor problem—the wandering dog—and got another—neighbors complaining about the fence. At first blush, you might think that everybody (again, everybody *except* dog owners) would be repulsed by dog feces.

Some people accept dog doo, along with litter, as an inescapable reality of urban and suburban life, not a preventable act. Generally, these people don't have gardens that are being defaced by dog feces, and they don't have small children whose small stature puts them in close proximity to dog doo. A fence is a reasonable, minimal, tool against animal toilet habits. And some sort of fence is probably legal in your community, especially if you can demonstrate that you have a dog problem. The most expensive stone wall or the least expensive chicken wire will work. For your neighbors' sake, if you do erect an antidog fence, keep aesthetics in mind. The more similar your fence is to other fences in the neighborhood, and the smaller it is, the better you will get along with all your other neighbors. How small? That depends on how good the dogs in your neighborhood are at jumping. Some dogs jump; others just bypass fences.

Invisible electric fences are marvelous inventions. They are relatively inexpensive and can quickly teach an offending animal where its world ends and yours begins. These fences work well for *your dog,* not your neighbor's dog. Electric fences, of course, do nothing to keep out dogs that aren't wearing a special collar. One veterinarian said, "My personal experience is that they work extremely well when properly installed and the animal's properly trained." For dogs, these fences work best when the animal first encounters the fence as a puppy. Some dogs (remember they're not all that smart) will go charging though the invisible fence, then not be able to return to the house. So if you do erect one, include a visible reminder that the invisible fence is there.

Cats wander too, and while they're generally not as big a problem as dogs, they can easily elevate themselves to the status of nuisance. Here's what one enterprising Nebraskan did about a cat problem:

*One of my neighbors (a retired widow who waters her lawn at high noon when the temperature is 100 degrees and "boils" my plants next to her yard in the process) obtained a "mature" cat a couple of years ago.*

*Well, several mornings last spring I saw Ms. Kitty scratching in my newly tilled garden and leaving me a present right where my carrots were to be planted (almost the same spot every day). So I just put up my "hot wire" fence around the perimeter of the veggie garden, and that took care of that little problem. Ms. Kitty doesn't come near my garden anymore, even though she still comes in the yard, which is okay.*

Electric fences don't harm animals. The shock they deliver is weak, but strong enough to teach an important lesson.

There are invisible solutions to dog and cat problems. There are a number of pet repellents on the market, made for people with your problems. Many of them are available in gardening catalogs.

But the responsibility for restraining the pets remains with the owners, right? You shouldn't really have to build a fence until you've exhausted your creativity in getting the owner to control his pet. And you can't fence everything. You can try talking to these people, but they will respond that penning an animal in is cruel. They didn't think Rover was a problem. Their dogs don't dig; their cats don't kill. The owners try to make you feel like an animal hater just because you want to be able to walk on your lawn without ruining your shoes. They try to make you believe that they have no alternative but to let their pets roam.

Sometimes you have to take an aggressive, yet clever, posture against dogs, as this Georgia resident did:

*I can't remember the people's name, but they were well known in their area for having a simply gorgeous yard. Green grass, beautiful flowers, well tended shrubs, etc. Their next-door neighbors, however, let their two large dogs run loose, and the dogs preferred to eliminate in the pretty yard next door.*

*After several months of asking the neighbors to please keep their dogs under control and various strategies to discourage the dogs from visiting, the lady started keeping poop in a box. She saved it up for about two weeks or so and then, on a Sunday morning (this was in the South, where everyone goes to church regularly, you know), she dumped it on their porch just outside the front door. They walked right out into it. The dogs weren't allowed to run loose after that.*

Dog owners usually don't get close enough to their pet's feces to appreciate how obnoxious it is. If a dog has inadvertently left its feces in your yard, well, then, you should return the dog doo to the rightful owner. Here's how one Washington state resident dealt with pooping dogs.

*One of our neighbors had an enormous dog who left enormous piles in several of our yards.*

*We got together and solved the problem by putting the resultant piles in small cardboard boxes, which we gift-wrapped. We have rural mailboxes set in rows here so it was easy to set the packages in the neighbor's mailbox on a regular basis. It wasn't long before the offending dog was put on a leash.*

Putting the poop through the dog owner's mailbox, on the owner's door mat, on the dog owner's newspaper—these are all ideas that have been used thousands of times a year by people fed up with having their yards become toilets. Returning dog poop is one of the first strategies that angry neighbors employ. It meets with mixed results, depending on that ultimate wild card—human nature. One reason that merely dropping poop off where it came from sometimes doesn't work is that neighbors who let their dogs wander usually don't care in the first place about civility, or they would keep their dogs leashed. A poop now and then isn't a big deal, especially if *only one* neighbor, you, is involved. But a gang of neighbors can make a much stronger point—and it's also a lot more poop.

If you do take the solo approach to leaving poop, be sure to include a note. You want to make sure that your neighbor doesn't miss the point. How could they? At 5:30 A.M., when it's time to walk the dog, there isn't a whole lot of cognitive power available to the dog's owner to evaluate why the poop is there.

Creativity counts. Some solutions to your neighbor problems involve yelling at your neighbor, calling the police, filing complaints with the appropriate department—all the regular stuff. Health departments take an aggressive stand against people who violate leash and dog poop laws—if they catch them.

It is the really inventive people who get results. Here's one inspired solution. A Cincinnati woman who had tried everything to keep free-running dogs from "littering" her little patch of garden, finally tried placing several of those plastic liter-sized bottles (soda bottles) filled with water, with a long cord attached around the bottle necks, and laying them in her garden. She claimed that it worked and kept the dogs out, so all of her neighbors followed suit. The dogs got tangled in the cord. Unfortunately, the dog owners were so incensed that their dogs returned home unrelieved, that they went and crushed all of the bottles.

Dog owners *rarely* acknowledge that their dogs are a problem. (They're even less honest about the menace they create than are the parents of small children.) Here's one situation, from Illinois, that's typical:

*My neighbor with the barking, messing beagle rarely heard the dog. But I did, right through my walls. I asked to have the poop scooped from my yard, so l could mow. She replied by telling me that she never heard her dog howl, that it only pooped in her yard (never mine), and that she didn't let it run loose every day, only three to four times a week! I finally erected a fence, at great cost to me. Three months later, she got rid of the dog.*

Denial is the first defense of dog owners. If your neighbor refuses to believe his pet is raising a ruckus, get some proof. Take some pictures and show the owner. Catch the dog in action: an indelicate bathroom pose, a garbage pose, a fight pose. If you can't get satisfaction from the neighbor, go public. That's what worked for one Baltimore, Maryland, man. He took his fight public by posting signs with the dog's photo. The sign said:

## WARNING

This dog has been seen unleashed, wandering the neighborhood, pooping on people's yards. If you see this dog, please call Animal Control. Dog feces spread disease, and are especially dangerous to children.

Everyone in the neighborhood knew who the dog was. The embarrassed neighbor collected her dog, Juniper, and kept him penned after that.

Roaming dogs are dangerous. While it's not the purpose of this book to delve into dog psychology, I just want to point out a few aspects of how dogs behave. All dogs have a boundary zone. When a threatening person or animal enters that zone, the dog will either run away or attack. Whether the dog runs away or attacks depends on the breed of dog and how brave that dog is. The size of this defense zone also varies. There's no way to know ahead of time what a dog will do when a stranger approaches. A small child who walks over to a roaming dog, intending to pet the animal, could succeed in his mission or could get his hand bitten. Without knowing about the dog, which event happens is a coin toss.

An untrained dog or one whose training has not been maintained is more likely to attack. But there's no way to tell by looking at the dog what its obedience level is.

Dogs respond aggressively to a wide range of activities. Running and yelling—things that children do all the time outside—can provoke a sudden, violent attack.

Virtually all localities recognize the potential danger of a roaming dog. Arizona State University enacted a strict leash regulation after three Seeing Eye dogs were attacked by roaming dogs. When blind students on campus asked other students to keep their dogs leashed, these sight-impaired students were shouted at. Penalties for letting your dog off its leash (which can't be longer than six feet) include stiff fines and having the dog impounded. In Tempe, Arizona, where ASU is located, the *criminal* penalty for letting your dog roam free can be up to $2,500, plus six months in jail. That's a law with more bite than bark.

Pasadena, California, has a similar law. But in that city you can also be fined for letting an unleashed dog run around your unfenced own yard. Why? Because a dog can suddenly change its mind and run into the next yard where there are small children. (Or dash across the street and get hit by a car.)

Letter carriers can—and do—refuse to deliver mail not only to houses with unleashed dogs, but to entire streets in which one dog owner has let his pet roam. The same thing occasionally happens to newspaper carriers. So if you don't get your mail or morning paper one day it might just be because one of your neighbors has let his dog wander.

Do leash laws really improve neighbor relations? Yes. In the first year that Orange County, California's leash law was in effect complaints against dog owners dropped fifteen percent; euthanasia of dogs dropped thirty percent.

Pets suffer, too, when their owners let them roam. One day King doesn't come home, and the next the owner gets a call that he's been killed out on the highway. Eventually, that's what happened to Juniper. The owner let the dog roam just once more, and that once more the dog was hit by a car. Sometimes the non-dog-owning neighbors get twice suckered. Once when the roaming pet digs and dirties. Then when they witness the pet being hit by a car, rush the poor animal to the vet, and end up stuck with the bill. Louise Anderson of Flagstaff, Arizona, had this story:

*A stranger's cat cost me fourteen hundred dollars, and it had to be put to sleep after a valiant effort to save it. I just finished paying off the bill. The cat's owner (whom I did manage to find) didn't offer a penny toward it, not even the "final care."*

What this story shows is how insensitive some pet owners can be, not only to their neighbors, but to their pets as well. A dog owner who lets his dog wander freely or a cat owner who never or rarely lets the cat inside may not care about that animal at all. In these cases, there's little chance that you'll convince the owner to restrain his pet.

Roaming dogs can do terrible things. Every dog is a "nice doggy" in the eyes of its owner, but dogs are unpredictable and can strike with sudden severity. Here's what one mother said about what happened to her child:

*My son underwent three and a half hours of emergency surgery the night of his accident, spent four days in the hospital being fed by IV, had approximately 300–400 stitches to his face, forehead, septum (inside his nose), outside bridge of his nose, under his nose, inside his upper lip, and a skin graft done on his cheek.*

In 1988 in St. Petersburg, Florida, a dog bit a six-year-old child. The child got an infection from the dog bite and died.

## CAT AND DOG DISEASES

Wandering dogs can sometimes get bitten by rabid animals, helping spread that fatal disease. Not everyone has their dog vaccinated against rabies, although all laws about it are strict.

Dog feces are dangerous, not to mention disgusting, especially when you discover it in your yard—and you don't have a dog. Rats enjoy dining on dog poop, so the neighbor who lets his dog roam and poop may be helping feed a rat family.

There are numerous diseases humans can catch from cats and dogs. The most serious is toxoplasmosis, a parasitic organism that's found in cat feces. In adults, toxoplasmosis causes flulike symptoms. A pregnant woman who gets toxoplasmosis has a 50 percent chance of causing a *serious birth defect* in her unborn child, including blindness and mental retardation.

Dogs sometimes carry hydatid disease, a worm-borne infection. These worms form eggs that produce giant cysts—the largest known contained twenty gallons of fluid—in bones and organs. The only way to remove them is through surgery.

Ringworm, a fungal infection, can be caught from both cats and dogs, though you're more likely to get it from a cat. Ringworm produces severe itching; it can also be passed from person to person. Cat *bites* can produce a variety of infections, and all cat bites require a doctor's attention. Children sometimes get toxocariasis, a worm infection, from dogs. In humans the toxocariasis worm penetrates the intestinal wall, enters the bloodstream, and then finds its way to the liver and lungs. In rare instances toxocariasis causes blindness. Children are most at risk, because they play closer to dog feces than adults do. Hookworms and roundworms can also be transmitted from dogs to people, say, by walking barefoot in your yard and stepping on dog poop.

Leptospirosis is another disease people can catch from dogs. It can produce jaundice or meningitis. Salmonella is always a danger from any animal's feces; it causes fever, diarrhea, and vomiting; young children, the elderly, and those with weakened immune systems are most at risk.

Wandering dogs can pick up tick-borne diseases, including, and most dangerously, Lyme disease and Rocky Mountain spotted fever

Whatever you do, don't give up. You have an absolute right to live dog-poop free. Dog feces equal disease. In no place is it legal for a dog to poop on somebody else's yard.

## Whom to Call About Roaming Pets

What's the law regarding roaming dogs and what they do to other animals? It varies from state to state, but this Georgia statute seemed typical:

*The owner, or, if no owner can be found, the custodian exercising care and control over any dog which goes upon the land of another and causes injury, death or damage directly or indirectly to any domestic animal which is normally and usually described as livestock or fowl, shall be civilly liable to the owner of the domestic animal or fowl, for damages, death or injury caused by the dog. The liability of the owner or custodian of the dog shall include consequential damages. The provisions in this section are to be considered cumulative of other remedies provided by law.*

In other words, it can be expensive for a dog owner to let his dog roam freely.

What if you don't want to spend five hundred dollars or more to build a fence? What if your neighbor simply won't keep his dogs penned in? What if your neighbor doesn't want to bother with a leash?—After all, it's much easier to let two golden retrievers walk by themselves, than try to restrain them on a leash.

When people get whopping mad, mad enough to fight—or worse—they often end up losing. TV actor Jameson Parker,* who starred on "Simon & Simon" was shot by his neighbor when one of his four dogs urinated on the man's lawn. For months, Parker's dogs had been leaving calling cards in neighbors' yards, and they had been complaining loudly. The trigger-happy neighbor was charged with attempted murder and assault with a firearm; it didn't help that Parker, his wife, and the dogs moved out of the neighborhood, because the neighbor now resides in prison.

The police aren't going to be much help. What are they going to do? Arrest the dog? Dogs don't like being put in police cars, and policemen don't like having to try to get them in. They're generally too involved with more important crimes to worry about wandering dogs. Dealing with dog problems is time consuming: first you have to collar the dog; then read the dog's collar. Then match the information on the collar with a name and address; then find the owner. In any event, when the police do respond, there's little they can do. Animal control or the health department is the avenue that's going to be most productive. Animal control is charged with the responsibility of dealing with stray and wandering animals. They're experienced and they know how the animals—and owners—will behave.

Every so often, depending on the phase of the moon, you may be awakened in the middle of the night by the lovely, heartwarming sound of cats in heat. Meowing at a volume that's almost too high to measure, at a pitch that's nearly high enough to shatter glass, cats call to each other.

* Real name

A major problem dealing with cats in heat is that at 3 A.M., it's nearly impossible to determine whose cat is engaging in the mating ritual. If your neighborhood has six tabbies (that you know of), and one of them is auditioning for the Metropolitan Opera, who knows to whom the cat belongs? Even if you did know, no cat owner is going to keep his cat in for those few nights a year that it's in heat, mostly because it's not possible to predict with any certainty what nights are going to be terrors.

My advice, then, is to deal with the cat the first moment you hear it. Have a water pistol handy (add a few drops of ammonia to the water), find the cat, aim, and fire. Do this *before* the cat has become comfortable for the evening. Bring along a bright flashlight or flash gun and frighten the cat. No harm will come to the animal, and, with the exception of these fifteen minutes, you'll get a good night's sleep.

The next day, you might mention to your cat-owning neighbors that there was a cat singing in heat all night long—did they hear it? A little guilt transfer will earn you points next time you need to ask your neighbor for a favor.

Perhaps the most significant way to calm a noisy cat is to have it spayed (females) or neutered (males). Like humans with cable television, when cats lose their sexual drive, they also cease to make a ruckus about sex. Spayed and neutered cats are quiet cats. Indeed, some localities require cat owners to spay and neuter their pets, unless they have a breeder's license.

Here's the ordinance from one California town:

*SECTION 2. Mandatory spaying and neutering.*

*A. No person shall own or harbor any cat or dog over the age of six months that has not been spayed or neutered unless:*

*1. The person holds an unaltered animal license for the animal pursuant to Section 4 of this ordinance; or*

*2. Guide dog puppies in training and police service dogs are exempted from the provisions of this section.*

*3. Any dog or cat over the age of six months adopted from an animal shelter in King County shall be spayed or neutered before transfer to the owner.*

If there's a neutering law in your town, mention it to your neighbor. Should your neighbor thinks it's cruel or wrong or too expensive to have his cat neutered, then let animal control deliver the message to him. If your town doesn't have a spaying and neutering law, now's the time to work to get one passed. There's no good reason why you should have to suffer through a night of yowling cats.

Pet poop can be a problem even when it remains on the owner's property. It all depends on the pet. Gus, a Vietnamese potbellied pig, like many others around the country, got a lot of attention. He's trendy, he's cute (humble too), and he's expensive. The Humane Society of the United States says pigs shouldn't be kept as pets because they need to wallow and root—messy, unsanitary behavior. Fortunately, lots of local laws ban farm animals from residential areas, though from Gus's point of view, the ban on residential pigs in Orlando, Florida, was the problem. Owners of the little pigs counter that at thirty-five pounds, they're smaller than many large dogs. And smarter too.

But maybe no one would have said a word if it hadn't been for the smell. It's not that the animal doesn't have tidy toilet habits, it's just that his owners are having a little trouble disposing of the waste. The pig is litter trained, meaning it buries its waste. Imagine living downwind. Pigs make a lot of poop, too: One pig owner disposes of twelve to fourteen 100-pound cans of waste a week.

Why mention potbellied pigs? If you do live downwind of a neighbor who's thinking of getting one—assuming you can find out ahead of time—be forewarned. You can stave off a big problem by trying to talk your neighbor out of getting this pet. It's possible that your neighbor isn't aware that potbellied pigs are so odoriferous: the literature promoting them doesn't point it out.

In addition to their calling cards, roaming pets leave other reminders of their visits. Dogs tear up your garbage. So do cats, but they're more dainty about it. Most of all, roaming animals harm other animals. If you feed the birds, you know what a problem dogs and especially cats can be.

●●●●●●●●●●●●●●●●●●●●●●●●●●●●●●●●●●●●●●●●●●●●●●●●●●●●●●●●●●●●●●●●

## LOBBY AGAINST PET PROBLEMS

Roaming dogs, potbellied pigs, aggressive cats got you down? Are these animals pawing at your garden, terrorizing your children, making your birdfeeder look like a saloon after last call? Then consider lobbying to change your local animal control ordinances. Some legislative objectives:

●

- Although most municipalities allow cats to roam freely, the Lewisville, Texas, animal control supervisor pointed out that laws requiring that cats be kept on their owners' property reduces rabies risks.
- Limits on the number of pets that any one household can have is another strategy. It's easy to be a good dog owner; it's nearly impossible to be a good dog owner of four dogs.
- Propose harsher penalties for unleashed dogs. Posting of signs pointing out those penalties can go a long way toward solving roaming-dog dangers.
- Have stringent penalties for dog bites. There should be no free bites; penalties should increase for each subsequent bite.
- Establish enclosed dog-runs, so that dogs can run around without a leash and without endangering children.
- Enact pooper-scooper laws.
- Enact noise ordinances that limit the decibel level that dogs can produce, either all the time or during sleeping hours.
- Permit only those cats that have been vaccinated and sterilized to roam freely.
- Require that ferrets be registered and vaccinated against rabies.
- Restrict potbellied pigs to nonurban areas.
- Clearly define what a farm animal is, and ban farm animals from residential areas.
- Forbid the keeping of exotic pets such as potbellied pigs, ferrets, raccoons.

Most changes in animal laws start because concerned or irate citizens are bothered by animals.

• • • • • • • • • • • • • • • • • • • • • • • • • • • • • • • • • • • • • • • • • • • • • • • • • • • • • • • •

Roaming dogs present an easier legal fight than roaming cats. Cats are considered feral animals, that is, their nature is to wander. Interpretation of the law is left to judges and juries, so the outcome of a lawsuit isn't always predictable. Here's one story from New York.

Cats don't just go after birds in cartoons; it happens in your yard. But if your yard is in a wildlife sanctuary, your cat had better not be the killer. A couple in Gates Mills, New York, wanted the killing in their yard to stop. It was their neighbor's cat that was doing the dirty deed. A black cat belonging to a couple by the name of Hurley was visiting the Clarks' property and killing birds. Hunting, trapping, and roaming animals are forbidden in the village, and police charged the Hurleys for letting their cat roam. The Clarks weren't cat haters. They kept their own cat on a harness when it was outdoors. But *that's* cruel, countered the Hurleys. The Clarks were serious friends of the birds. Melanie Clark was a volunteer rehabilitator for the Lake County Metroparks, and she took home sick and injured birds to nurse them back to health. She tracked the movements of hawks and other species she saw in her yard and sent the information off to Cornell University.

The Clarks keep birdfeeders that attracted several thousand birds a year. And, as they like to point out, household cats cause at least 20 percent of the injuries at the Metroparks Wildlife Center where Melanie Clark volunteers.

In their defense, the Hurleys admitted that although a black cat might have been killing birds at the Clarks's feeder, it was not their cat. Like most pet owners, they said, "Not my animal." They said she never left their yard. The Clarks insisted it was not so. The matter went before a judge, who decided in favor of the Clarks.

• • • • • • • • • • • • • • • • • • • • • • • • • • • • • • • • • • • • • • • • • • • • • • • • •

### PERIPATETIC PETS

Take action against the pet's owner, never the pet.

Better yet, take pictures.

Start a poop collection for the pet's owner. Drop off your gift when the neighbors are entertaining.

Get in touch with your neighbors who are gardeners. They're likely not to be too keen on a neighbor's pet pooping in their yard.

Get in touch with the parents of young children. Animal excrement and kids don't get along. You'll find allies among parents.

• • • • • • • • • • • • • • • • • • • • • • • • • • • • • • • • • • • • • • • • • • • • • • • • •

## TOO MANY ANIMALS

Sometimes you wouldn't mind one dog or cat, but some people just can't stop once they start collecting anything.

Here's what happened to one St. Petersburg, Florida, homeowner:

•

*First let me say that I own a cat; it's a mouser. I have a neigh-bor two doors down who has about thirty cats! There are several howl-ing cat fights every night, and the cats steal my cat's food. They were constantly spraying everywhere, cat crap all over our lawns and occa-sionally even on the hoods of our cars, on the stairways, and even on my neighbors' front-porch bar! And that bar is about twenty-three feet off the ground! (We live in stilt houses in a beach community.) After explaining things to the cat people several times and having animal control come out weekly to trap the critters, I went out and bought a Havahart® raccoon trap. We were averaging 1.5 cats per day and were getting to know the entire staff at animal control on a first-name basis, when we found out the guy was coming onto our property and taking them out. The cat man then kept all these felines in the house with him, that is until they could no longer stand it. More trapping ensued. Last week the cat man built a cage about 4'x6'x8' in his back-yard and stuffed as many of them as he could in it. He still sneaks onto our property whenever one of the @!#$%! things is missing.*

Sometimes when the animal control officials won't (or can't) act, you have to do what you can. And people with thirty—or just five—pets are, well, a bit eccentric. They'd sooner cut off their right arms than to part with a single animal, so don't even bother asking. (If you don't think they're a bit kooky, just look at their wills.) In many less-than-urban localities, local law may permit people to have as many pets as they wish. The only way to thwart these mass-animal owners is to try another approach. Are the animals a health threat? If so, see what your health department can do. Are the animals noisy? Then local noise regulations may be violated. Is your neighbor *breed-ing* animals? If so, he may need a license. Are the animals being treated cruelly? Contact your local humane society. Animal control is only one of many potential agencies that can bat in your favor. Government bureaucracy is so varied and so large that if you explore a little, you find just the agency that you need. (Hopefully.) If they seriously bother you, you need to move, see an allergist, or sound-proof your house. Oh yes, and plant lots of fragrant flowers.

The following story seems like a bad joke. A family in a Denver suburb had 105 poodles, although local ordinance permitted only 3 dogs. When someone turned in the owners, who were dog breeders, they faced a choice: move or get rid of the dogs. They took a third option: they got a dog-law lawyer and fought. (The lawyer had once represented a Chicago area couple with 140 poodles, speaking of overspecialization in the law).

The couple had moved into their home in the early 1960s to engage in poodle breeding, before the law was enacted; only later was the area annexed into a suburban town. No one complained until 1991. The judge let the poodles stay.

The moral: Even in what seems like the most outrageous case, you can't count on achieving victory through the law. This case also speaks to a general principle when it comes to dealing with annoying neighbor pet tricks: act swiftly. You don't have to take instant, irrevocable action against the neighbor with the annoying pet. *But you do have to make your opposition clear from the moment you learn about the animal.* Time favors the status quo. (This general observation is true for other annoying tricks neighbors perform.)

If the pets were in place before you appeared, you may simply be stuck with them.

Paul and Martha Rogers wanted to enjoy their retirement in a country setting. Their neighbors, who were there first, said they just wanted to make a living. The problem was, they operated a dog kennel.

Of course the Rogerses fought with a lawsuit. Kennels are always controversial: they're noisy and sometimes even smelly. As with other controversies, the themes in this fight were familiar. The Rogerses said they had to stuff cotton in their ears to get any sleep. The Van Vorsts, the people who owned the dogs, pointed out they were there first and operated a business that had never caused any complaints in seventeen years. The county even gave them a permit to expand their operation to keep seventy-five dogs, doubling their capacity. That's when the Rogerses started to complain.

The Rogerses lost. Keep this important point in mind: If you are considering moving into a neighborhood with an animal problem, don't count on being able to eliminate that problem once you've moved in. The odds are not necessarily in your favor.

But there are people who had it worse than the Rogerses. What about roaming farm animals? Robert and Nancy Disson were gardening in their front yard when a goat attacked them. They lived near a house that some neighbors had turned into a farm.

Another neighbor had hung double windows to block out the noise. Everyone in the neighborhood was used to the occasional stray chicken. But a goat? It was an upscale neighborhood, but the

•

barnyard was there first—since 1967. Surrounded by homes selling for $175,000 to $200,000 was a farm, belonging to Barnaby and Althia Wittaker, an elderly couple who had kept chickens, ducks, sheep, goats, and horses since before there was a subdivision. In 1990 the neighbors filed a lawsuit against the Wittakers.

The neighbors had a lot to complain about. Obviously the farm reduced property values; it was poorly kept and relatively unattractive. The odor that emanated from it was a little stronger than the smells that came from the other neighbors' ovens. It attracted flies and other insects. The fowl didn't stay put and often defecated on neighbors' cars. And then there was the noise. The Wittakers spent thousands of dollars for their legal defense—and won.

While this book is about winning the war, it's important to point out that not all wars are going to be won. It's also important to know this ahead of time.

So what do you do when the law is on the side of the animal owners? You take frequent vacations, use lots of perfume, move your air-conditioning condensers to the other side of the house, buy double thick windows. But mostly you wait.

Just because the law allows people to keep animals, it doesn't necessarily allow their animals to be a nuisance. If you're attacked by a goat, bring that matter to somebody's attention. If a wandering dog trespasses and frightens your children, call animal control. If a chicken uses your newly waxed car as a toilet, make a stink in court. Or catch the chicken and have a nice supper.

You may lose the war over animals, but you and your neighbors can also win enough battles to make it very tiresome for the animal owners. Tire them out. Use guerrilla tactics and attrition. One small claims court case every now and then isn't going to matter; but if a dozen neighbors file suits twice a year, the animal-owning neighbors may decide it's not worth the trouble to keep all those critters.

• • • • • • • • • • • • • • • • • • • • • • • • • • • • • • • • • • • • • • • • • • • • • • • • • • •

## FIGHTING THE NUMBERS

See what laws the owners are breaking. Give them a chance to settle things themselves before you call the law.

Discuss noise abatement projects.

Try a variety of devices to exclude or frighten the roaming animals.

You and your neighbors can fight many small battles, and,
over time, these small battles can result in your winning the war.

• • • • • • • • • • • • • • • • • • • • • • • • • • • • • • • • • • • • • • • • • • • • • • • • • • •

## THE BETTER TO EAT YOU WITH

What happens when your neighbor collects poisonous snakes? What
if you think the neighbor's pets are dangerous? Often there's not
much you can do unless a local law is on your side. People who own
fierce animals are religiously devoted to them. They are often fierce
themselves. These people don't care what you want. They don't even
care what every neighbor thinks. They want their pets, if you can call
them that.

What if you lived next to these guys?

Two brothers near Ottawa had the neighbors a little riled over
their pets of choice: cougars and wolves. The wolves and cougars
were smelly, noisy (the wolves howled at night) and worst of all, as
the fairy tale goes, had very, very sharp teeth.

The two brothers and their menagerie ended up outside Ottawa, because they had had to leave their previous residence in Wa-
terloo, Canada, quickly after one of the cougars clawed a boy. No
matter what, the brothers were determined to keep their six pets
(three of each).

If the neighbors should eventually succeed in forcing the wild
animals out, one brother threatened revenge. "I'm going to bring in
pit bulls and Rottweilers and paint everything fluorescent orange."

Neighbors like this are as dangerous as their pets. The safest
way to deal with them is to ignore them. Teach your kids not to play
around the animals, and keep an eye on your children at all times because they'll try to do it anyway. And then keep protection close at
hand always; a cayenne-pepper–based spray made for protection
against bears is one option. If your neighbor keeps really dangerous
pets, then you might consider getting a gun and learning how to use it.

Strange neighbors with dangerous pets have to cooperate in
some small ways, so your neighborhood won't be a, well, complete
zoo. These neighbors still have to obey the law, and most cities and
towns forbid keeping wild animals as pets. Even those that allow
such animals in private homes still have nuisance laws to keep noise
and odors to a minimum. When you smell or hear something un-

pleasant, call the owners (keep the number by your phone). That may calm things down for a little while.

In Clearwater, Florida, a green-wing macaw was the problem. This bird was so loud and aggressive, said one neighbor, that it was "almost like a Doberman pinscher that was going to attack you."

In Warrenton, Virginia, the problem was pit bull terriers. That's pit bulls in the extreme plural. How would you like to have three dozen pit bulls living next door? That's what Jewel Metta had. Imagine trying to barbecue with thirty-six pit bulls growling and barking as you turn the burgers. So Metta's neighbors called the local animal control board. Health officials. Zoning officials. Trouble was, there was no violation.

What? No law broken? Hard to believe, but it was true.

And Metta didn't regard her dogs as especially fierce.

Keeping dangerous animals isn't necessarily against the law. Once they bite or kill somebody—that's against the law. In the meanwhile, do the best you can and protect yourself. If you feel that an animal is a menace, you are right. The definition of a dangerous animal is one who makes people feel afraid.

Sometimes people moan and groan about threatening animals, but they never actually do something about a dangerous animal in the neighborhood until it's much too late, usually after some sort of casualty.

In this case, even though neighbors thought two dangerous dogs were roaming the neighborhood, no one took action. And a tiny dog died. Sometimes a name is destiny. Taco, a Dade City, Florida, Chihuahua, was killed by two larger dogs roaming the neighborhood. His owner had released the tiny dog in his yard, a presumably safe place, and had gone back indoors, when a yelp alerted her to trouble. She saw one of the large dogs carry away the small dog. Although neighbors had complained, rather gently, about the roaming large dogs, nothing had ever been done to control them. Animal control told neighbors to file a civil suit, something that didn't interest them. The killer dogs' owners were charged with keeping vicious animals.

It could have been worse—these dogs could have killed a child. To the owners, however, the dogs were as gentle as pussycats. That's usually the case: most dogs treat their *owners* well. "He won't bite." That's what they all say. Not infrequently dog owners just don't care if their dog is vicious. Sometimes the trespass and damage are habitual. And someone finally takes notice too late.

A woman by the name of Sue Mehl in Georgia's Polk County lost her poodle when the German shepherd next door came into her yard, killed the smaller dog, and stole his bone. It wasn't the first time the shepherd had trespassed; in the past the dog had destroyed two pairs of Mehl's shoes, five outside doormats, and had repeatedly overturned garbage cans and strewn garbage all over Mehl's lawn. Each time, Mehl visited her neighbor, Al Penney, who did nothing to restrain his dog. In the end, the two wound up in court with Penney paying Mehl two hundred dollars in damages.

Merely complaining doesn't always produce results. But don't let this story keep you from trying. In Ohio, Felix Fleming asked neighbor Richard Archer to refrain from walking his dogs while the Fleming children were waiting for the school bus. The dogs were habitually interested in knowing what the children smelled like, and neither the children nor their parents enjoyed that. The situation escalated into a classic neighbor war, with Archer accusing the Fleming children of teasing his dogs and Fleming accusing Archer of harboring vicious animals. The families wound up in court, and in the end Archer moved.

......................................................

## ADVICE WITH TEETH

Make your concerns known to the pet's owner. Show the owner newspaper articles in which neighbors were awarded judgments in lawsuits. If that does nothing, talk with as many appropriate officials as you can. See if the animals are violating any laws—business, sanitary, noise—whatever you can discover. If nothing else, your complaints make for a stronger case if you end up in court.

Keep kids and the vicious animals far apart.

Get some protection in the form of pepper spray, or whatever you consider appropriate.

Always remember: any dog can maim or kill.

......................................................

# 8

# Property Wars

Property conflicts begin in the playpen when a child first learns to say "Mine!" or "No!" and they continue through life. So they should come as no surprise to folks who argue over access, boundaries, or fences.

People come to blows over a three-inch trespass of a driveway, they scream at one another about who should paint the fence. But fighting and yelling are for sissies. Tough neighbors sue. Many property disputes end up in the hands of judges and juries. So take your lawyer by the hand and read on.

One word of caution, though. People believe that private property is sacred. They think trespassing is a capital offense; and they mete out the penalty. In San Jose, California, a man shot a neighbor because the neighbor's dog had urinated on that man's Sunday newspaper.

Of course, there had been a prior dispute going on between these two neighbors, so the wet newspaper wasn't entirely responsible for the death. These two neighbors had been fighting over a parking space for years. Once the killer neighbor let air out of the other neighbor's car. Once he smeared dog feces on the car's steering wheel. But it was all about who can do what on whose property.

## BORDERS

What belongs to whom? Who owns the tree on the border? Your neighbor says your driveway infringes several inches on his property—do you need to resurvey? As North America gets more crowded, people are arguing more about smaller and smaller pieces of land. After all, when you pay a half million dollars for a home with a tiny yard, every inch counts.

First, the bad news. A tree on the border belongs to both neighbors and they must be able to agree about what is to be done with it. You both have to agree to plant it in the first place. And if your tree grows so much that its trunk straddles the property line, your neighbor gets part ownership. Seems unfair, but there's little (I won't say *nothing*) that you can do. So if you want the tree to go—or grow—your neighbor has to agree.

Now if your neighbor's tree overhangs your property, most jurisdictions give you the right to cut that part of the tree, as long as the cutting is done from your side of the property line and you don't enter your neighbor's property to do it.

Cutting first and discussing later is not a good idea, but it is your right if you choose to exercise it. Because you have a right to remove the offending branches from above your property, you have absolutely nothing to lose by talking about the problem with your neighbor before you take action. After all, it's not going to be a secret who did it.

The Washington state judge had it right when he said that no jury could force people to become good neighbors. He was talking about two neighbors in particular—one had erected a long fence between himself and his neighbor so that he didn't ever have to see his neighbor. But neighbor number two complained that neighbor number one had cut down ten of his fir trees in the process. Harassment suits followed, then countersuits—as a result, the lawyers were tens of thousands of dollars richer.

Trees are a nexus for property disputes of all kinds. Some neighbors want their neighbors' trees cut down; other neighbors want their neighbors' trees to stand forever because they create shade or block noise; still other neighbors just want those trees—the way thieves want wallets. In fact, people often help themselves to their neighbor's trees, especially in sparsely populated areas.

When Paul Ligon contracted to have a logger selectively cut his 173 acres of forest near Buffalo, New York, he was surprised to find someone had already beat him to the job. A neighbor had contracted with a timber company to cut trees down; the timber company made a mistake and cut trees on Ligon's property, ruining the stand for years to come. Ligon filed a civil suit against the logger and his neighbor in which he claimed that they harvested 164 of his trees. The timber company had taken incredible liberty with boundary interpretations. They trespassed fifty to one hundred yards onto Ligon's property to remove the trees, including valuable maple, ash, tulip, basswood, cherry, hemlock, and beech.

Timber thefts are especially common when a neighbor is pruning his stand; it's tempting to cross the boundary to get a valuable tree. With good trees bringing several hundred to as much as a thousand dollars, it's tempting to grab a few no one will miss. Boundary trees are especially vulnerable, even though both neighbors in theory must agree to cut them. Poorly defined boundaries complicate the situation. Over time property lines become blurred. When ancient property lines were defined by trees and other natural landscape features, it's easy to see why boundaries can be in dispute.

Property and tree conflicts escalate (like any neighbor dispute can). Take the case of the Trumps and Saatchis,* Chelsea, England, residents. William Trump claimed Saatchi vandalized a Charles II chestnut tree. Charles Saatchi claimed Trump hurled racist remarks at him.

It all started when Saatchi wanted to renovate his Georgian mansion, and offered £5,000 to all his neighbors for their troubles. (Now that's the kind of neighbor I could like.) In short order, Trump

* Real Name. This is the Saatchi of advertising fame.

had filed a £95,000 lawsuit claiming that Saatchi's renovation had damaged his property.

From then on, the property war escalated. Saatchi, according to Trump, installed stadium-sized floodlighting, aimed you-know-where. Saatchi claimed that Trump had vandalized his cherry tree. One day Saatchi's Rolls-Royce caught fire, while parked, although there was no evidence of how the fire had started.

Ah, the lifestyles of the rich and famous.

What can you do to prevent your good neighbor from becoming a tree thief? The first step is a recent survey. A good survey is worth the bother and expense, especially if you give your neighbor a copy. Giving your neighbor a copy of your survey doesn't have to be done in a threatening manner, or even with any sly implications. Just say, "George, would you mind keeping a copy of our survey for me? I'm worried about fire, and it would give me peace of mind if I knew you had a copy."

The major difference between wars between nations and battles over neighbor borders is that nations have the ability to draft soldiers; neighbors have to pay for their soldiers, who are called lawyers. Neighbor feuds usually get more television coverage, too. Both kinds of conflict can be bloody. Most of the time the matter of who owns what is solved simply. Both neighbors agree to pay for a surveyor whose verdict is more or less final. To satisfy future generations, the surveyor can place boundary markers in the ground— you and your neighbor pay for these, of course. When you and your neighbor make an accommodation on the boundary, hire a lawyer and get it in writing. Your grandchildren will thank you.

On the other hand, property disputes aren't *always* resolved so easily. Sigh.

Name-calling doesn't help when it comes to resolving property line disputes—or any neighbor conflict.

Two Washington state neighbors would sneer at each other when they spied one another through their kitchen windows. These two families had been feuding over their property line for years. Finally, they brought their case to a mediator, and the conflict was resolved when one neighbor agreed to stop calling the other "hippo butt."

•  •  •

•

.............................................................................

### WHAT'S MINE IS MINE

Bite the bullet and have your property surveyed.
When you think you've been violated, speak up immediately. Your neighbor may just be misinformed.

.............................................................................

## EVENTUALLY, IT'S NOT A WAR, IT'S A NUCLEAR CON-FLAGRATION

Property-line disputes are often the nastiest. Except, possibly, for
parking disputes. When property and parking disputes are com-
bined, well . . . read on.

This is the case of John Weatherly versus Sam Williams of
Pinellas Park, Florida. Before I write about the "why" I want to reveal some of the "what." It's a long list, so I'm going to offer only
some excerpts.

- Williams reported to the sheriff that Weatherly was building
  a fence without a permit.
- Williams reported that Weatherly was building a back porch
  without a permit.
- Williams reported that Weatherly was building a swimming
  pool with a false contractor's license.
- Williams told Social Security that Weatherly was employed
  while collecting disability.
- Williams reported to the sheriff that Weatherly dumped cat
  litter onto the street.
- Weatherly reported to the sheriff that Williams dumped dog
  feces onto the street in the same location.
- Weatherly complained of vandalism (and so did Williams).
- Williams complained of verbal abuse (and so did Weatherly).
- Weatherly reported that Williams was pouring toilet water
  into his yard.
- Weatherly reported to the sheriff that Williams's dogs were
  barking too loudly.
- Weatherly complained that Williams painted a car in his
  front yard.

- Weatherly complained to the postal authorities that Williams tampered with his mail.
- Weatherly reported that Williams searched his garbage.
- Weatherly sprayed Williams with a garden hose. (This is the only act that either of the two admitted. Williams, who is blind, was walking his dog one afternoon. At that time, Weatherly was watering the patch of grass on the sidewalk near his house. Williams had to cross the sidewalk; Weatherly told him to go around or walk through. Williams walked through, got wet, and called the sheriff.)

The fight had not yet *begun* to get nasty.

But let me go back to the beginning. What could cause such animosity between neighbors?

The central issue (though there evolved many other issues) had to do with a the property line between the Weatherlys and Williamses. When Sam Williams bought a rather large trailer he also bought a dilemma: where to park it. From Sam Williams's perspective, the best place was in front of his house. Said Williams, "I listen to talking books in there. In the house, the phone is ringing, the dogs are barking. It's like an extra room where I can get away."

So far, so good—right?

Williams parked his trailer in the driveway between his house and John Weatherly's house. Every time Williams opened the trailer's door, the door banged the fence. But, according to Williams, the fence was his, so he just removed it. Aha, not so, said Weatherly, who maintained that the fence belonged to his son. In addition, Weatherly said that Williams parked his trailer over a foot inside Weatherly's property line. Maybe, maybe not. But the story doesn't end here. Weatherly also contended that every time Williams got out of his trailer he flattened the grass on Weatherly's property. So Weatherly built a new fence, absolutely on his property and with a nifty feature (from Weatherly's point of view): the fence prevented Williams from opening his trailer door. Weatherly's fence was three feet tall, sixteen feet long, not attached to anything else on Weatherly's property, and clearly there for one purpose only: to keep Williams in or out of his trailer, but not both. Williams moved his trailer, dubbing the fence the "go-to-hell fence."

That's when the antics really began. Williams escalated the war that summer by sending a letter from "Citizens for Decency in

Bonnie Bay," in which he chronicled Weatherly's criminal behavior. The letter said that Weatherly "is considered dangerous around juveniles. If you see any suspicious behavior, please call the Sheriff's Department. Let us all pull together to rid our neighborhood of this filth and protect our children."

A follow-up letter claimed that Weatherly was a child molester and pornographer, not to mention "slime." Let me point out that Williams, in fact, had denied sending these letters but had admitted trying to get neighbors to picket Weatherly's house because he lived across the street from the local middle school. Williams did say that after receiving the letters he checked on Weatherly's criminal record and indeed discovered that nine years earlier, when Weatherly lived someplace else, he had pleaded guilty to "involving a minor in a harmful motion picture."

During the dispute Weatherly had two neighborhood children, aged seven and seventeen, in his house. When Williams found out he called the FBI; a child abuse investigator was dispatched. Williams has also told the neighbors that Weatherly's twenty-two-year-old girlfriend was eighteen when they started dating, pointing out that Weatherly seems to have a "thing" for young girls.

This dispute is far from over. It may never be over for as long as these two men live. Weatherly is suing Williams for slander. Williams's defense is that what he's said is the truth. Weatherly's attorney says the truth, distorted or real, can't be used to launch a vendetta. One neighbor said about the whole affair, "I'm about ready to go down there and tell them to knock it off, to stop acting like little boys."

No doubt you or someone you know has been involved in a property war. If there's to be any hope of reconciliation, or at least of resolving the property line war, then it is imperative that you keep the dispute focused on the issue. If you sense in your bones that escalation is in the offing or if your neighbor starts to escalate the conflict then *immediately* seek a mediator. Once bad words have passed between your lips and your neighbor's ears it is nearly impossible to prevent a chain of events from occurring that will consume your life. Not every property dispute escalates to the level of nastiness that the Williams-Weatherly dispute did, but on the other hand, some become worse. It's easier than you suspect for a conflict to spread out of control.

Property disputes and hard economic times go hand in hand. That's because money can sometimes solve neighbor problems, but during recessions many people have less money to spend that way. For example, money that someone might spend on a fence to deal with a neighbor's roaming dog just isn't there. And people become more insular, more concerned about protecting their property: they worry about keeping its value up. We are territorial animals, whether we admit that fact or not. Encroach on my land, and I'll get mad, even vicious. To some degree, people can control the value of their property—or if they can't, then they certainly won't let you do anything that diminishes its value.

The denser the population, the more intense the territorial disputes. Suburbanization of rural areas, urbanization of suburbs, and superurbanization of cities makes this an even more acute problem.

Property conflicts are often the most divisive. How much have you invested in your home? It's probably your most important asset, and you protect it for all you're worth. You protect it from the would-be evil government, and the would-be evil neighbor. When confronted with a danger to your house, you don't compromise. You fight like a cornered dog. And to the death. Or until you can no longer afford to fight.

Harry Olivieri mortgaged his house to pay his legal fees, but after losing in court to neighbor and adversary, Pat Rachford, he is considering an appeal.

It all started in an argument over an easement. The Rachfords said the Olivieris harassed them, watched them, called and hung up. The Olivieris said the Rachfords hurt their dog, poisoned their trees, and harassed them because they're Italian.

Lots of property wars start because people don't really understand what their neighbors are saying. They talk and don't listen. To keep things perfectly clear, and to make your neighbor know you are perfectly serious, you should put things in writing. When you really want something from your neighbor, it's hard not to hear exactly what you want to hear. We get consumed by our own myths. That's probably at the root of the following dispute.

The story of Barnaby and Barbara Ingersol and Steve and Nan Post reads like a case study of what not to do. In the end, the Ingersols sued the Posts for damages they sustained for abuse of process.

•

A jury awarded the Ingersols $7,350 compensatory damages and $50,000 punitive damages. The Posts appealed from the judgment entered on that verdict and lost.

It all started in February 1975, when Steve Post, a licensed Arizona attorney, filed a complaint against the Ingersols in Maricopa County for breach of an alleged oral contract, fraud, and defamation. Post claimed the Ingersols agreed to share the cost of building a retaining wall on the Posts' property but adjacent to the Ingersols'. The Ingersols would have been liable for $780.69. A dizzying list of counterclaims and countercounterclaims followed.

The court imposed sanctions against the Posts for obstructionist activities. Then, before the case could come to trial, Post moved for a continuance of the trial because, as a lawyer, he was committed to represent a client on the same day. The Ingersols pointed out that Post wasn't the counsel for the case. Post countered that he was indeed representing the case. At one point, Post claimed he had a tape recording of conversations between the Ingersols and Posts agreeing to co-payment for the wall—proof of the oral contract that could prove perjury by the Ingersols. Post wanted the tapes sealed and protected.

On closer questioning, Post admitted the tapes were blank. The court then dismissed his complaint and awarded the Ingersols five hundred dollars in attorney's fees incurred on their motion to produce and their response to appellants' motion for protective order, plus their total court costs incurred in that action.

Not content to let things stand, the Ingersols sued the Posts for abuse of process by using the courts to harass them and subject them to excessive legal fees. Throughout the proceedings they said Post told them he could break them with legal maneuverings and make their lawyer rich.

A totally ridiculous fight, right? Escalation occurs very quickly in property disputes. There's hardly a homeowner who hasn't done something wrong, who hasn't violated some local ordinance, who doesn't have something to hide. Get involved in a no-holds-barred dispute and you can be pretty sure that your neighbor will dig some of this stuff up.

Property disputes don't all come from misunderstandings. Sometimes the offending neighbors are just sneaky and conniving. Take the Colorado family who built their home so that the snow on their roof slid off onto their neighbor's roof. Colorado, for those who don't live there, gets a lot of snow—several feet a year. The snowed-on family got their neighbors cited for city trespass, and the new-roofers had to pay to rebuild the roof.

Some neighbors consider property lines to be an inconvenience, one that they really don't think they can be held to. Take the case of one swimming pool owner:

*I understand that swimming pools are a lot of work and have therefore had little interest in having one of my own. I had noticed for a while that when my neighbor was cleaning the pool he would skim it, add the various solutions, and finally clean what I thought was a filter by leaning over my fence and dumping whatever into my shrubbery. It bothered me but I didn't say anything until I had removed the shrubbery and put in a perennial garden which I believe to be more sensitive than the shrubs to these chemicals. He continued the process until I asked him not to do it anymore. The response was that it was nothing but water and it wouldn't hurt my garden. I suppose he chose my yard and not his because mine is closer to the pool, but if it was only water surely he could have dumped it in his pool, which is even closer than my yard.*

• • • • • • • • • • • • • • • • • • • • • • • • • • • • • • • • • • • • • • • • • • •

## KEEPING YOUR HOME AND YOUR MONEY

Make written agreements any time you and your neighbor share responsibility for common property like plants, trees, or structures.

Before you build near or on your property line, talk to your neighbor.

Hire a good surveyor.

• • • • • • • • • • • • • • • • • • • • • • • • • • • • • • • • • • • • • • • • • • •

## BEWARE THE SQUATTER

Hey, the nice man next door sure keeps that strip nicely landscaped. You know, the strip of land on the other side of your driveway adjacent to his land. He sits in his lawn chair there too to enjoy the flowers. Just hope he doesn't lay claim to it. It can happen.

•

In 1965 Allan Carr and his wife bought a home in Bristol, Massachusetts, and lived there quite contentedly for twenty-two years while their children grew up. For the entire time Carr openly used a strip of his neighbor's property adjacent to his own land. Carr kept the strip mowed, planted a garden there, built a fence, maintained a white board fence, trimmed and trained hedges, planted a red Japanese maple, and hosted countless picnics and cookouts with his family. The neighbor, Fred Bayard, neglected the remaining part of the land that Carr didn't maintain, but he took a sudden interest in it in 1987 and had the property surveyed. Then he discovered Carr was trespassing on his property. Carr notified Bayard that he now owned the property by *adverse possession,* a practice that awards land to someone who uses it openly as his own for a period of years.

Bayard, angered by his loss, took things into his own hands, and over a three-day Columbus Day weekend destroyed what Carr had created. He had his men cut down everything green on the property and removed the fences. He then put his own fence up on the property line of record and poured asphalt where there was once lawn.

When Carr sued, the courts agreed that the fifteen-foot strip of land was his by adverse possession. Since the judge found Bayard knew about Carr's adverse possession at the time of his fit of destruction, they fined him for damages for a total of $37,886. In addition, the court found Bayard would not be entitled to any back real estate taxes or rent for use and occupancy of the land.

It happens all the time. Even to famous people. Former Beatle George Harrison* owns a lovely estate on Maui. And for years his neighbors have used a trail over the estate to access the ocean. Because the path passes near his home, he blocked access to it with a locked gate. But his neighbors sued, and a judge agreed that they were guaranteed access through the property because the path was a well-established access to the ocean, in use for years.

The angry Harrison threatened to move, and he can certainly afford it. But not all of us can. That's why you have to be careful about letting others use your land. Let snowmobilers ride on your property year after year after year and pretty soon they'll have the right to do it even when you no longer want them.

The law of adverse possession is old and established—and should be well known by now. But still people get caught by it year

* Real name.

in and year out. Sometimes they're not even aware they've lost the property and sell it to someone else when it belongs to the squatter. Buyer beware.

In 1930, when April Spencer and her husband bought their home in Washington, D.C., a scrawny chicken-wire fence designated the boundary with the house next door. One of Spencer's first tasks was planting rosebushes, well to her side of the fence. Over the next sixty years, other rosebushes joined the first on a thirty-inch-wide and five-foot-long strip of land, which grew into a charming rose garden. All that ended in 1989 when a young couple, the Treelands, moved in next door and showed her a deed that put the roses on their property because the boundary was on the other side of the strip. Then they put up a fence that captured some of the rosebushes.

So Spencer sued, and a D.C. superior court judge found the strip to be hers by adverse possession. Since Spencer had tended the roses and taken care of the land as her own for much longer than the required fifteen years, it became hers.

Before going to court, the Treelands made every effort to compromise. The young couple tried to negotiate a solution. They offered to pay to have the bushes transplanted to Spencer's yard. Then they said they'd cut a gate in the fence to give Spencer access to her roses. They wanted to give her possession of the land until she dies, when the land would revert to them. But Spencer wanted what had been hers for sixty years. And the judge gave it to her.

• • • • • • • • • • • • • • • • • • • • • • • • • • • • • • • • • • • • • • • • • • • • •

## WATCH YOUR BORDERS

Check boundaries closely before buying any property.

When you find trespassers, order them off your land. Make it official. Call the police and post No Trespassing signs.

Consider posting Radioactivity Area or Warning: Radioactive Waste Buried Here. That often does the trick.

• • • • • • • • • • • • • • • • • • • • • • • • • • • • • • • • • • • • • • • • • • • • •

# RIGHTS-OF-WAY AND EASEMENTS

My family and I share a driveway with our next-door neighbors. At the end of the driveway between our two houses are two garages, one

•

for each of us. The deed to our house, and to our neighbor's house, gives both of us right-of-way through the driveway. That means we all have to keep the driveway clear so that everyone can get cars in and out of the garage.

In practice, neither of uses our garage, at least to park cars. The garages are too far from the houses, and besides, garages are great places to store junk! What we do instead is park our cars in the driveway close to our respective houses. The cars block access to the garages, but that doesn't matter.

From time to time, contractors park in the middle of the shared driveway, preventing us, or our neighbors, from getting in. My wife and I are extremely lucky that our neighbors are so considerate; when they can't get into their driveway because of one of our contractors (or a guest), they simply park on the street. And we do the same. So although neither of us is obeying the easement as prescribed in our deeds, we don't have any property line squabbles.

But that's not the case with the Markses and Abotts, who share a driveway not too far from our house. Their shared driveway also is an easement to their garages. But Kurt Abott turned his garage into an extra bedroom, so he had no place to park his car. Except in the driveway.

When Abott put his car in the driveway, Rodger Marks couldn't get in or out without first ringing Abott's doorbell. Not a convenient situation. This led to more than a few shouting matches. Although the deed prohibited Abott from parking in the driveway, he did anyway. One of the reasons this became such a problem is that the first few times it happened, Abott was so nice about being such a jerk, and Marks was so nice about Abott being a jerk, too. After Abott had parked in the driveway for a few weeks, there was (at least in his mind) a tacit understanding that he could park there all the time.

The moral: If a neighbor is violating your property rights, make your wishes known immediately. If you let your neighbor use your property (or shared property) as his own, put a time limit on how long it will be allowed. Otherwise, the neighbor will assume that it's okay to continue, and you'll simply fume more and more until tempers fly.

This particular conflict between the Markses and Abotts had some even sorer spots. Abott was an architect, and worked in his house. From time to time his clients and assistants would drop by and park—you know where. Did I mention that Rodger Marks had a one-year-old daughter who waited, screaming, in the car while her daddy made arrangements to have the driveway cleared?

A couple of summers ago (when all this started) the Markses went to Maine. When they returned, they found Abott's car parked not in the driveway, but on their lawn. All I can say is it's a good thing the Markses went away for only a month and not an entire year. Otherwise they might have found squatters in their house.

Treat encroachments on your property promptly and sternly, but in a cool, polite manner. If you share a right-of-way with neighbors, talk about how you all plan to use the right-of-way. In the Markses' case, there was no plan. (Abott probably didn't think very long about what he would do once his garage vanished.) In my case, my neighbors and I had a plan that differs from the legal requirements spelled out in our deed, but which works quite well.

# 9

# Slob
# Neighbors

Neighbors with ugly yards, junked car collections, deteriorating roofs aren't fun to have living next to you. Junk-pile and slob neighbors become particularly loathsome when it's time to try and sell your house. Nobody—well, almost nobody—wants to move next door to a family that collects rusted vehicles or just collects rust. Anybody who is willing to move next door to a mattress graveyard certainly has the upper hand in bargaining over the price of a house. If, in the name of neighbor relations, you've put up with your neighbor's front yard being a laboratory of oxidation experiments, then, when you want to sell your house, it's time to blast away the problem.

The first step, as always, is to talk with your neighbor, unless this course looks too risky. Speak softly, because people have a hard time yelling at someone whose voice is just barely above a whisper.

Follow up your conversation with a nice note, one that expresses gratitude to your neighbor for getting rid of their collection. Never call it "junk"; many people are fond of the stuff, or view messy yards as normal yards. Don't try and bully your neighbor—egos usually prevent that tactic from working. Because nobody wants their property values to decline, you might assume that it should be possible to get many people to clean up their yards, but I don't think that's true. Some families *prefer* their property values to stay low while they're living at their house. Higher property values mean higher taxes, so the less their house is worth, and the less *your* house is worth, the better off they are. This can be a significant financial impediment to your getting a more scenic neighborhood. And some people just plain don't care.

## YARD WORK

Yard-slob neighbors are not the worst of all evils. In fact, you might just *want* to have a slob as a neighbor. Why? Consider the alternative: somebody who is obsessively, compulsively neat; somebody who either nags you about cleaning or who guilt-trips you into cleaning. Here's the reasoning as explained by one Michigan homeowner:

*The phrase "keeping up with the Joneses" can probably be traced all the way back to the Civil War. I live in Marquette, Michigan, where we accumulate over two hundred inches of snow every year, and I once had a neighbor who was compulsive about shoveling.*

*Starting as early as 7 A.M., Bill hit the concrete, eventually scraping and tossing his way down to pavement. His driveway and sidewalk were snow- and ice-free throughout the winter.*

*When I first moved into the house next to Bill's, I was irritated by his obsession. Armed with only a scooped shovel, he managed to do what many gas-powered throwers can only attempt. Bill was retired, and therefore had the time to nurse his compulsion. I would leave for work, backing out of the driveway with wheels sliding and spinning, and manage a "plastic" wave and smile to Bill, leaving my driveway for that evening.*

*One night I came home to find that Bill had done my stretch of sidewalk as well. I suppose that's what made me crack. My driveway was certainly shabby next to his, which bothered me, but now this re-*

*tired man had started taking on my domain as part of his daily devo-*
*tion. It was probably an ego-based, macho "thing"; however, the next*
*morning I was out with my shovel at seven. Bill had started at six-*
*thirty. With the next snowfall I was out at six-thirty, only to find Bill*
*halfway done. I now was able to jokingly confess that I was out to com-*
*pete with him, that I had accepted his challenge to have the best win-*
*ter driveway in the city. One evening in March, we received a*
*seventeen-inch dumping (with drifts of three feet against garage*
*doors). I could have called my brother-in-law, who had a plow. I*
*could have borrowed a snowblower from the guy across the street.*
*No . . . I couldn't have done these things, because Bill was down to*
*pavement by six forty-five. I invited him in for coffee, which he turned*
*down because he didn't like the effects of caffeine! Grabbing my red*
*scooped shovel, I went out into the driveway, and started pushing,*
*scooping, and tossing. Before I was halfway down the twenty-yard dri-*
*veway, I was already one hour late for work. By nine-thirty, I was no*
*longer able to move my right arm—I'd dislocated my shoulder.*

*"Any trouble, Jim?" Bill asked from his front steps, which he*
*was salting down.*

*"No problems here, Bill, though I think I'd like a wider shovel."*

*I stubbornly pushed on, finishing the job. I got into the van and*
*drove to the Emergency Room, where they treated my shoulder and*
*tied my arm in a sling.*

*That was three winters ago. I have now developed tendinitis in*
*the right elbow and have had to switch from a shovel to a "scoop,"*
*which is a thirty-inch-wide sheet-metal bucket that is pushed through*
*snow. I have no problem getting up as early as four-thirty in the morn-*
*ing in order to have the drive cleared, and have developed a wonder-*
*ful sneer for the late risers in the neighborhood who power their labors*
*with fossil fuels. I am somewhat blind to their impressions of me, how-*
*ever.*

*Bill is dead, and the new neighbor handles his snow by driving*
*on it over and over and over. All that really does is pack the stuff*
*down, though. I ought to go over and advise him about how to use a*
*red scooped shovel, perhaps even offer some assistance. I could take*
*care of his sidewalk. I don't think he'd mind.*

When you mow, shovel snow, trim bushes, and cut branches,
you have to put the yard debris somewhere. Most people place this

stuff out on the street for the city to pick up, or else they haul the trash away themselves.

But not everybody. There's an easier way. Take this story, for example:

*I have a friend who lives in an older part of town. The houses are cheek by jowl with the driveway extending along the side of the house. His neighbor's house was set farther back on the lot than his house, with the result that on one side of my friend's driveway was the side of his own house but the other side of the driveway was his neighbor's lawn. For the first part of the winter my friend would push the snow to the front of his driveway and throw the snow on his own lawn.*

*As the winter progressed, his lawn was covered high with the snow and there was nowhere except his neighbor's lawn to pile the snow. Relations had deteriorated to the extent that the first shovelful of snow brought the enraged neighbor out, and while one was cleaning his driveway, the other was cleaning his lawn and throwing it on my friend's driveway.*

*We can laugh about it now that my friend has moved to a new area, but it wasn't funny at the time.*

Many communities have rules about keeping lawns, raking leaves, and so forth, so you may have the law on your side. It's worth a call to the appropriate local enforcement bureau if talking directly to your neighbor doesn't work. Any effort is worth encouraging, so be sure to notice when your neighbor does something to clean the yard up. Cities view sanitation fines as a lucrative source of revenue, so don't deny your municipality extra income.

If you suspect your neighbor isn't able to take care of his yard—and the yard's lack of upkeep drives you nuts—offer to do it yourself in an offhand way. "Since I have a riding mower, it's just as easy to do your lawn when I do mine. It's no problem." But you may find yourself doing it every other Sunday.

If your neighbor has too many junk-pile sculptures in his yard, make this offer: "I'm getting rid of my dead washing machine to-day—hauling it off to the dump. Can I take yours along, too?"

. . .

.

•••••••••••••••••••••••••••••••••••••••••••••••••••••••••••••••••

## NATURAL SLOBS

Hire a kid to keep the slob's yard neat.

Be willing to compromise. You'll probably have to be happy with a yard that falls somewhere between the Everglades and the Bronx Botanical Garden.

•••••••••••••••••••••••••••••••••••••••••••••••••••••••••••••••••

## JUNK AND TRASH

Slob neighbors usually don't restrict themselves to just one area of sloppiness, say, leaving their trash out. Usually, the tendency is to be a slob as well as you can. For instance:

*My neighbors don't throw trash in my yard; they throw it in their own yard, where it blows into mine regularly. They seem to feel that one must warm up a car for no fewer than fifteen minutes, but thirty is closer to the usual time spent on this task.*

*Last year they had some friends over in October and when I woke up the next morning the pumpkins that they had stacked up in front of their house were in my front yard. (I should have taken them—might have taught them a lesson.) They have a riding lawn-mower (this for one-third of an acre) with headlights, so if they "need" to mow late (read 9:30 P.M.) they can. I don't imagine they'll say anything bad about my gardening. All the weeds I spent all of last summer rooting out of my yard (bought the house last year) came over the fence from their yard.*

*One time last summer, one of my cats went over the fence (all backyards are fenced with six-foot wooden privacy fences) and I had to climb up on ours to get her back over where she belonged. I saw why she wanted to be there. They mow paths in their backyard around piles of junk!*

And the prize for keeping a sloppy yard and sharing it with the neighbors goes to this slob:

*All this pales beside my experience with neighbors who kept a*

*fishing boat in their backyard and threw their crab and fish debris in
our backyard all summer.*

But in some cases, the problem may be as simple as your
neighbor's not knowing how to get rid of that old refrigerator or car.
People often don't know where their local landfill is, or they miss the
semiannual bulk pickup that the sanitation department makes.
Show those neighbors the light! Guide them down the golden path to
the landfill! Offer to help. If you get a positive reaction, that's a good
sign. If the neighbor is unwilling to part with his treasure, maybe
he's at least willing to hide it. If you agree to help him move a particularly bulky item to his basement or enclosed garage, you might
inspire him to do more cleaning himself. Might.

When you're trying to sell a house, it may be worth spending a
few dollars cleaning up your neighbor's place. Treat your neighbor to
a cleanup, and consider it a moving expense.

When being nice and helpful doesn't work, it's time for step
two: forceful action. When your junk-pile neighbor has resisted all
sensible forms of communication, speak to him through local ordinances and regulations. In every community there are laws against
turning your property into a junkyard. The degree of cleanliness
varies from one locality to another, but be assured, there are government officials who are willing to write tickets and take your
neighbor's money if he doesn't clean up. It may be possible to
snitch on him anonymously, although he'll probably know who did it
if you've complained to him before. But it never hurts to keep your
name off the official record. In any event, your other neighbors will
be grateful that you've taken these steps to improve the neighborhood.

However, not everyone hates junk neighbors:

*I admit my neighbor is a pack rat. He's a recycler, and I'm
amazed at what he finds in the trash. You name it; it's in his yard.
Garden statuary. Garden plants. Vinyl tablecloths. Ladders. All sorts
of garden tools. Cans of paint. Lawn-mower parts. Bikes. Barrels.
Treasure, pure treasure all arranged in neat piles. One day a red canoe appeared there, and when I asked a few questions, he let it be
known he was willing to part with the craft for under fifty dollars. A
red fiberglass canoe. A seafaring canoe. He threw in a can of red paint*

·

*and a patch kit, and I ordered paddles and life jackets from L.L. Bean. And I was ready for the high seas.*

I love living next to this guy. He has several yard sales every year. One time I picked up a KitchenAid mixer (retails for over one hundred dollars) and a portable crib (ditto). He keeps a great garden, and he rototills the neighborhood gardens for free. He can fix anything. I wouldn't trade him for the cover neighbor from House Beautiful. I hope he never moves.

Maybe you can make the best of your junk problems, like this woman. You never know when you'll need a ladder. That's one way. A pretty fence is another.

Junk problems are visual ones. Unlike noise, your neighbor's junk won't (usually) jump a six-foot privacy fence. Building a fence to ease those eyesores is sometimes a bittersweet experience:

*Fact is that my too-close neighbor is a hermit. I only know what he looks like under a streetlight, as he never leaves his house when the sun is out.*

*His backyard was once upon a time littered with scrap lumber, bricks, abandoned bits of lawn furniture, an old stove, and a 1970 AMC Hornet. These days you can't see much of that, for all the weeds and vines left alone for the season. A ball that strays into Tim's backyard is quickly given up for lost.*

*Three months ago, I realized that talking with Tim about his yard was not going to accomplish anything. The site is an eyesore for the entire neighborhood and is especially one for me. I decided to build a privacy fence.*

*The fence is sixty-five feet long, and five feet high. It holds 223 vertical cedar slats, each screwed to one of 23 eight-foot two-by-four cedar support rails, which are attached to one of 13 four-by-four cedar posts. The posts are eight feet long, buried three feet deep.*

*As I was slowly making my way down the property line, slat by slat, I began feeling an odd combination of pleasure and impatience. I would catch myself chuckling, comparing my deed to that of Montresor and his bricks.*

*Strolling couples would remark on how nicely the fence was coming along. Some would ask why it took so long to start. Tim remained in hiding. I drilled the final screw home in the base of the final slat, and surveyed my work. Since I am not very mechanically inclined, this was my first solo home improvement project. It had taken me a week of afternoons and one and a half Saturdays to complete.*

*It's been two weeks since I finished, and the fence I've built is tall and reasonably straight. After a rain shower, the entire yard smells of fresh cedar. Happy is the owner and builder of a new fence.*

*I am beginning to miss Tim, though.*

More often than is desirable, an entire house is junk. The Toronto city government wanted to tear down Bobby Waitkins's house and have him pay for it to the tune of $68,000. Waitkins's house was a junk house, with no heat, defective wiring, mice infestation, and more; the front yard piled with all sorts of stuff including rusting, abandoned cars, batteries, auto engines, damaged furniture, and even food.

The neighbors said that living next to Waitkins was hell. One neighbor with a small child said his child "is just starting to walk. But we can't let him go outside. It's too dangerous."

The neighbors and city finally won the fight. But this particular battle had been going on since 1968; the demolition order was issued twenty-five years later.

• • • • • • • • • • • • • • • • • • • • • • • • • • • • • • • • • • • • • • • •

## ONE MAN'S JUNK

Make the best of the situation.
Offer to have some especially large trash hauled away.

• • • • • • • • • • • • • • • • • • • • • • • • • • • • • • • • • • • • • • • • •

## ANTI-SLOBS

Then there are those people who can't stand any mess, who take great offense to anything you do that defies their sense of neat and clean.

For example, take Phoenix resident Barry Feidler, eighty-one, who reported his neighbors for property maintenance violations eight times in the past three years. Feidler's favorite reading was the city's maintenance code book, which he kept handy at all times. "Whenever I see something I don't think is right I'll call the inspec-

•

tors up," he said. What constitutes sloppiness in Feidler's eyes? An unsightly trailer, clothes hanging to dry beneath an awning, grass that's too long. To Feidler's credit, he did try to talk with one neighbor about the mess, once: "And I won't do that anymore. He got madder than hell and told me it wasn't any of my business."

Which, of course, it wasn't. But despite the fact that none of his neighbors would talk with him, Feidler said he'd continue on his crusade. "Once one of them gets by, the first thing you know," Feidler said, "the whole neighborhood is botched up. Then you can't sell. All you can do is pack up and leave."

Hey, now that's a good idea.

There's little you can do to defend yourself against a neatness fanatic. In Feidler's case, not even all his neighbors could rally change in the man. Eventually, the city inspectors, the judges, the police, all recognize a fanatic. Eventually.

# 10

# Weird
# and
# Uncivilized
# Neighbors

N eighbors vary wildly in three levels of weirdness and civility. Consider the man living in the Sierra Nevadas who fires his gun into the air from time to time to attract his neighbors' attention so that he can tell them his hunting stories.

Neighbor problems can often be greater than the sum of their parts. Frequently, broad, serious issues are involved—not just for the people involved, but for the community at large. Not all neighbor conflicts are funny or even benign. Some are deadly serious, with serious consequences if mishandled. What if your neighbor works for organized crime? How do you deal with a racist neighbor? One San Pablo family handled that problem this way.

Rather than acquiesce or even move, Robert Cary, an African-

American, initiated a civil rights lawsuit against his neighbor, Stan Gray. Mr. Gray had threatened violence and used racist epithets against the Carys. Mr. Gray, in fact, had recently been released from prison—where he had been put because he made violent threats against the Carys. Gray had thrown dog feces in the Carys' yard and poured oil in their swimming pool, among other things. On one occasion Gray told Mr. Cary: "I'm KKK. I'm a Nazi and so are my friends. We're all active KKK members and I'm going to hold Klan meetings right here in the court, right in your front yard. We'll drive you out with our meetings." The Carys won a large (though undisclosed) monetary award from Gray; the court also issued a restraining order against Gray: He was prohibited from coming within a half-mile of their house or their daughter's school, and had to stay at least one hundred feet away from any of the Carys on the street. In addition, Gray had to perform 150 hours of volunteer work at the NAACP. The Carys' lawyer put it this way, "My clients put their foot down and asked why they should have to move."

One mean husband and wife used to hop on one foot whenever they saw their neighbor, who was a Korean War veteran and had only one leg. This couple also displayed pornographic posters in their window and played loud music early in the morning. It took fourteen months to get the couple evicted from their apartment.

It may take you some time to decide if your neighbor is a harmless weirdo or a dangerous one. I don't have advice for dealing with these people other than: Watch your back and keep your distance. Well, that and get to know a reliable real estate agent.

## WEIRDOS WHO THINK YOU'RE THE PROBLEM

A Minneapolis assistant city attorney knows of one man who has made more than a thousand complaints against neighbors over the past several years, usually about trivial offenses most people wouldn't even notice. Houses next to the man's home have been sold repeatedly as people move to escape his carping.

## THREATENING AND SCARY MONSTERS

Most of the tales I have to tell in this chapter are of a cautionary nature. There really aren't many morals here, other than that life can take strange, barely sane turns, and you should proceed with humor and caution. I hope you are somewhat amused by these stories, and I hope that, regardless of how awful your neighbors are, what you read here makes you feel that things could be worse. Much worse.

Remember the Davis family of Albuquerque from the Noisy Neighbors chapter? This was the family with eight children and four Rottweilers that pooped all the time in the yard. The Davis family spent most of their spare time yelling at one another. Occasionally, they let their Rottweilers roam, and when they did, these dogs chased neighborhood children. To defend their dogs from irate and threatened neighbors (do Rottweilers need defending?), the Davises waved baseball bats. More than once, the police intervened. The Davises were moved into the neighborhood by the city because they were homeless, and they were homeless because their previous house had burned down. Why did Mr. and Mrs. Davis have to move into this particular neighborhood? It was a condition of their bail. They were out on bail for arson.

You can't worry too much about your neighbor's feelings when your family's well-being is at stake. That's what this New Yorker decided:

*This is about a house we owned upstate which we lived in briefly and now rent out. It is part of an old bungalow colony in the Catskills and most of the population just used them to summer in but when the recession took hold, a lot of people winterized to live all year long.*

*At any rate, we had several wonderful summers where we escaped from the city and went up to our quiet mountain retreat until our neighbors moved in. They are an ex–Hell's Angels couple who took in a foster child with severe problems. The guy himself is scary-looking, very verbal about his racist sentiments, and they also have four dachshunds who yap continually. But let us remember, they are the full-time residents.*

*We got a great deal on some stockade fencing, as the property line on one side was a little too close to them. I later happened to overhear him talking to the mailman and anyone else who would listen (actually I think he waited till he knew I was nearby) about the fence.*

•

*He was derisive and I think angry, but he never did say anything to us.*

*There have been other unpleasant incidents, such as the time he dug up and jury-rigged terracing that eroded onto our property, etc., but the fence episode was the one that was most vivid in my mind. I kind of felt bad—it was not my express purpose to hurt him or block him out personally (though I can't say I intended to become close buddies), more just to have privacy so our daughter could run around the yard freely without dogs or anything else bothering her.*

Sometimes there is simply nothing you can do about a neighbor. Some people turn into Jim Joneses—others stay borderline, and, well, it's in your interest to keep your neighbor from crossing that line. Take the case of a engineer from Oregon whose neighbor thought he was killing her roses and dogwoods with laser beams. The case was brought to the attention of a mediator, but the mediator failed. (Naturally: the mediator had to be some kind of alien.) You can go out of your way to avoid riling people whose neurons aren't that well connected, but they always find a reason to take offense.

People with paranoid tendencies tend to turn on nearby targets—like their neighbors. And they imagine complex conspiracies set up against them. Sometimes it takes time to decide if your neighbor is a harmless eccentric or a dangerous psycho. New Yorker Dexter Cahn's downstairs neighbor accused him of stealing precious artifacts from him and posing as an FBI agent to try to trick the neighbor into spilling the beans. But Cahn wasn't guilty. His neighbor also tried to leak gas into Cahn's apartment, once broke his car windows, chased Cahn's twelve-year-old son down the street, and verbally harassed Cahn. Cahn got some peace when the man was committed to a state mental hospital.

It's true—crooks have to live somewhere. And that somewhere might just be next to you.

There are degrees of crookedness, for we are all, at one time or another, guilty of something illegal. If your neighbor dumps toxic waste in forests for a living, well that's bad and criminal and he should be in jail, but despite all that he might be a good neighbor. It's when a neighbor's crookedness haunts your house that there's a real big problem. Eliza lived next to one such person:

*Chris and his wife sold their house to a couple whose name I don't remember. They were about our age (late thirties) and had a five-year-old son. They were cheap—or poor—depending on how you look at it. She wore seventeen layers of clothes in the winter, never turned the heat on. He had no "real" occupation, worked at all sorts of odd jobs, among which was delivering of the Sunday* New York Times. *He always had many copies left over, so for about a year we luxuriated in free copies. We always thought he sold other things too, like pot, but we never knew for sure.*

*Perhaps this accounted for their kid, Alvin. Alvin was totally undisciplined, and very smart. He thought nothing of wandering into your house and raiding the fridge. During the year that these folks lived next door, our food bills crept up by about thirty percent. It took us a while to figure out why, since we worked for a living, and weren't around to see what was happening. (Didn't we lock the doors? Sure, but this little tyke was clever as hell—he suckered in the lady who tended our baby while we were at work, she must have thought he was ours, too).*

*Anyway, we caught on when he strolled in at six o'clock one Saturday morning, acting as if he owned the place, which by then I guess he did. If it hadn't been for the cat's objections to his confiscating her dish, we might not have noticed.*

*When we, uh, politely complained to his mother, she said, "Well, he didn't steal anything valuable did he?" No, we had to admit. Unless you count the cat food, and if she didn't care, then why should we?*

People who use their houses to run their business can be particularly aggressive about defending their turf, not to mention their livelihood. So be forewarned: If your neighbor's business is in his house, not only is there little you can do to stop him by way of gentle persuasion, but he might work to persuade you to stop your persuasions.

In a village outside of Addleston, England, a man sold used cars from his backyard. The neighbors didn't mind (too much) that George Sue pursued his vocation; they just wanted him to keep things tidy. But Sue objected vigorously to any advice his neighbors gave. He spray-painted his neighbors' cars. He poured superglue on his neighbors' cars. He broke their headlights. He threatened to burn their houses down. One neighbor said, "It has been a misery living near him. He threatened to kill us and have us all out." Years of torment, but there was nothing the neighbors could do, because there was no proof.

Finally, one neighbor went to visit George for a chat, carrying a weapon for defense—a fork. In court, the neighbor testified, "The next thing I knew was that he threw me on the ground in the yard and he hit me with the fork. He shut the gate and said to me, 'You'll never get out of here alive.' He struck me with a fork on my forehead on the right-hand side. He struck me with a brick on the back of the head."

George was finally convicted of malicious wounding. Oh, and by the way, George was forty-two years old; his neighbor was eighty.

There's always going to be one better. Few are better (that is, really worse) than what happened to Mitchell Kline, who lived in Takoma Park, Maryland. Things got so bad, so out of hand, that the Kline family moved out of town. But those are my words—here's the story as told by the person who lived it:

*We spent three years battling noisy, law-breaking, gun-shooting, trash-strewing neighbors and emerged without so much as a Pyrrhic victory. You might say that our tolerance was the loser.*

*The house was a charming, Spanish-style bungalow in Takoma Park, Maryland, a suburb of Washington, D.C., known variously as "The People's Republic of Takoma Park," "Tacky Park," and "Where Old Hippies Go to Die." It was our first house.*

*What we didn't know when we moved there in 1990 was that the slightly run-down Cape Cod-type house across the street was owned by the most notorious slumlord in Takoma Park. "Gimpy," as our other neighbors uncharitably called this limping West Virginian, had divided the tiny house into four apartments, none of which had adequate plumbing, heat or electricity.*

*Gimpy stuffed this warren of rooms with a changing cast that included a prostitute, a pair of single welfare moms (sisters with a gaggle of kids), about a dozen Mariel Cubans, and various tattooed, bare-chested white men whom (we discovered later) were generally on the lam.*

*The latter group of drawling chawbacons included Dante, a slick-haired, thirtyish fellow who ran the corner Laundromat. ("You can't beat the commute," he said). Dante's hobby was playing his banana-yellow electric guitar alfresco. Like the lead guitarist in Spinal Tap, he knew only one volume setting: eleven, on a scale of ten. His fairly broad repertoire of blues and rock was unfortunately all played to the same chord changes: "Louie, Louie." Occasionally he was joined by a gent who played electric organ with all the skill of a key-*

*punch. Their vocals recalled something from a hospice.*

*The former group included Robin, a twenty-fiveish woman whom we called "the Fishmonger" for her raspy and bellicose voice. Once I literally heard her from two blocks away ululating for Wayne, her plug-built, slow-witted nephew: "W-HAYYNNA-HHHHYYYYYH-H-H-H." The Fishmonger spent the summer of her pregnancy preparing like any conscientious mom-to-be. Every night, from about ten o'clock to 2 A.M., she would entertain gentlemen callers on the tailgate of a Jeep parked next to our driveway and about twenty feet from our bedroom window. They weren't doing the horizontal hop; they were just sitting, smoking Marlboros, and drinking Iron City beer, then flinging the cans and bottles against the curb. During the day, Robin always had something to say, as well as the amplification equipment to broadcast the message, which was never true. "HEY, I'M CARRYING TRIPLETS FOR MY HUSBAND, WHO'S OVER FIGHTING IN DESERT STORM," she'd report from the next telephone pole down the street. (She later delivered a single baby girl.) "I'VE GAINED SEVENTY-TWO POUNDS SO FAR."*

*But it was the middle group, the Cubans, who caused the most fretting and sleepless nights. They were a dozen or so men, shabbily dressed and always coming and going in any of a half-dozen different customized vans and pickup trucks, none of which had proper mufflers. Some had license plates of cardboard and scrawled numbers. Yet we could never get the cops to tow.*

*There was not a woman in sight. These men never seemed to work but employed the vans and trucks to haul in an unbelievable variety of trash, mostly appliances large and small. We don't know what they did with this stuff. Each week it would wind up curbside, lining the width of the property. Since the Cubans never paid attention to the actual day of trash pickup, we looked every day at rusting hulks of refrigerators, fans, metal furniture and other oddment. The food trash went out at random, too, encouraging Takoma Park's only wild dog pack to turn our street into a collage of chicken trays and fast-food wrappers.*

*We called this group, uncharitably, the Carumba Brothers. When they spoke, it was even louder than the Fishmonger, but with a good deal less clarity. I speak fairly fluent Spanish and could never understand a word. The Carumba Brothers stood around nose-to-nose constantly jabbering "AY-ARR-AY-AR-AH."*

*Like everyone else across the street, the Carumbas played loud,* live music outdoors, drank, and peed on retaining walls. There was also something menacing about them. Unlike Dante or the Fishmonger, they were aloof, returning our occasional greetings with glares, and slipping furtively in and out of their driveway in the vans. They regularly staged brutal fights. I once saw two beating each other with what appeared to be lead pipes. Another time one pitched a twenty-inch TV tube off the front porch. It landed on the pavement with a spectacular blast. There was something vaguely superhuman about the Carumbas, too: they'd sit out around a card table in boxer shorts on subzero nights, be up carousing at 6 A.M. after having drunk themselves into trances only hours earlier.

The Carumbas also kept chickens, which I think they ate, and one rooster, who tortured the whole neighborhood for months. This rooster didn't wait for sunup. Each morning he'd start crowing from three-thirty on. And he was a free-range rooster. Some mornings I'd be curled into bed with ear plugs and pillows over my head, trying to escape the inevitable caw, when the beast would leap on our windowsill and crow directly into our faces—from two feet away.

There was noise during the day, noise at night. Guitars, B-Bs, choruses of "Cielito Lindo," donnybrooks verbal and with fists, breaking glass, and the cock crow. Even when my neighbors weren't making noise, I'd often lie awake waiting for the next affront. Then I'd fall asleep (pass out, really) on a stack of papers at work. "New father," my colleagues would say. "No, my daughter has been sleeping through the night for months. IT'S MY NEIGHBORS!" When I did sleep, I'd have dreams about circus geeks and arson. I was desperate, exhausted.

I tried everything to get rid of the rooster. First, legal means. I called the city and they said they could do nothing: "We laid off our animal control officer four years ago," said the voice on the phone. "You mean it's legal to keep barnyard animals here?" I asked in disbelief. "Then I'm getting a cow today," I told the anonymous voice on the telephone. I considered poison but worried a cat or dog would eat it. I spent one entire Saturday afternoon trying to chase the cock into oncoming traffic. It was too smart. It would simply run in circles around a parked car. Or drivers would brake while I'd be waving my arms and screaming, "Don't stop! Hit the gas! C'mon, STOMP IT!"

Around the same time the rooster simply disappeared, another neighbor reported he found a bullet from a 22-caliber rifle lodged in his doorway. Tom had taken a fishing rod, stuck it in the bullet hole, *and deduced that the trajectory indicated that it had come from "that house across from you where all those Italian people live."*

*It was time for some real action. We called a block meeting with our beat cops, the police captain, and our city councilman. They were sympathetic. The beat cops said they would check on the slum house every day to try to keep the peace. They'd even bring along a Spanish-speaking social worker. The police captain spoke about the criminal history of the residents, which was long, violent, and outstanding (Dante, among others, had long before skipped town). The councilman said that the county and city had a legal bead on Gimpy the slumlord. He had been fined thousands of dollars. And he would be required to convert his illegal apartment back into a single-family house. Or else go to jail in contempt of court. That probably meant that Gimpy would have to sell to some decent, renovation-minded family. "It should all be resolved within sixty days," he said.*

*Well, it took about ten months and resolution came, but not as our councilman had promised. As we packed our moving van on a gorgeous spring day, the Fishmonger came by to wish us well. The Carumbas were out drinking beer, revving their engines, and probably wondering where to get a good deal on a new rooster.*

Life could always be worse.

## ANNOYING HABITS AND HOBBIES

When does your neighbor's hobby cease to be an amusement and become an obsession? And what happens when that obsession becomes your personal hell?

The closer you live to your neighbors the worse your neighbor problems can get. This problem was particularly awful. It's about birds. From the outset let me say that I happen to like birds and not only that, but I've written three books about bird feeding. So I have a positive attitude toward our feathered friends. But what happened to this one college professor was particularly chilling.

Imagine these circumstances: At six o'clock every morning you awaken to the sound of pigeons crashing into your window, pigeons cooing on your windowsill. Pigeons don't arrive alone, or even in affectionate pairs—they arrive in loud, unruly flocks.

"Suddenly, I was awakened one morning by the noise of birds

crashing into my bedroom window." The professor, Claire McCloud, sent a note to her upstairs neighbors, John and Sarah Brissie, who were feeding pigeons and who were the cause of the problem. In typical New York City fashion, where you don't talk to your neighbors, the Brissies responded with a note saying that they would take care of the pigeon problem. The pigeons didn't go away, however. Then one day, Professor McCloud's bedroom window was shattered by a shot from a pellet gun, presumably from some concerned citizen just doing his part to reduce the pigeon population.

Professor McCloud was obviously concerned that she might be shot through her window. She contacted the building manager who put bird repellent, a sticky goo, on her windowsill. The pigeons went away—most of them, anyway.

Then one day Professor McCloud received a complaint from the ASPCA, informing her that the Brissies had reported that Professor McCloud was poisoning pigeons and other birds. The ASPCA investigator examined her windowsill and concluded that the repellent was too thick and it was killing birds. At her request, the manager put on a lighter coat of repellent; yet Professor McCloud continually received threatening calls from the Brissies and the ASPCA investigator that she was killing birds. A month later, while Professor McCloud was away, the ASPCA obtained a search warrant and entered McCloud's apartment to photograph her sill. A couple of months later another ASPCA officer and several police officers burst into Professor McCloud's office and arrested her for cruelty to animals (as well as for resisting arrest). She was escorted from the university in handcuffs and thrown in jail for four hours.

Three months later all charges against Professor McCloud were dropped. As you can imagine, the professor was whopping mad, real mad, as mad as somebody can get. She is currently suing the ASPCA and the Brissies for four million dollars.

Sometimes you can't win. In a Washington, D.C., apartment building there lived an elderly woman who was known in the building for not being completely aware of her surroundings. One morning, for example, she was found walking around the halls in her underwear. Months later, somebody on this woman's floor smelled gas coming from her apartment. (The woman left her door ajar, secured by the door chain.) The good neighbor called the fire department, which arrived in force. After the fire department had relit the pilot light on her stove, the woman thanked the anonymous neighbor with a big note posted in the hall that said "TO WHOEVER CALLED THE FIRE DEPARTMENT: BUTT OUT!"

Most of the time bird feeding is an innocent hobby. But some bird feeders are passionate about their hobby almost to the point of being terroristic. I'm absolutely certain of this, having talked with hundreds of bird feeders over the years. It's a wonderfully delightful hobby, entertaining and educational. But birds are messy, loud, and generally unschooled in etiquette. They do rotten things to recently waxed cars and backyard decks.

The same is true for most animals—they don't give a hoot about cleanliness. If a neighbor has more than one animal and those animals are not domesticated, there are bound to be strange consequences.

Few neighbor conflicts turn deadly, but they can. People become obsessed with their conflict—they can be relentless, pursuing victory (however oddly defined) until both their enemy and they are destroyed. Take the case of one Miami, Florida, man who hated his neighbors because their dogs chased his cats, they played music too loud, and they parked on his property. He added thallium nitrate, a poison, to a few bottles of Coca-Cola, and then managed to get the bottles into his neighbors' refrigerator. He killed one of them and sent two others to the hospital. This neighbor was sentenced to death for first-degree murder.

If your neighbor acts oddly, he probably is odd. Be leery.

A simple feud between two Plant City, Florida, neighbors ended when one neighbor, who was seventy-two years old, shot another, who was sixty-three. Nobody knew exactly what their dispute was about, but it's certainly over now.

I don't think that Florida has any weirder, more dangerous neighbors than other states, but here's yet another Florida case, though this one is a little less bloody. A Brooksville, Florida, man was arrested and charged with frequently dumping trash in his neighbor's yard. The neighbor logged seventy-nine instances of dumping before calling the police. He had also set up an all-night video camera to record the misdeeds. Ultimately, however, the case was dismissed against the garbage dropper because the amount of trash didn't meet the city's minimum weight requirement for becoming a legal violation.

On reflection, one element of Florida's demographics may make neighbor problems more acute in that state. Florida has a large population of retired people. Elderly, retired men and women, who are home much of the day, have the opportunity to become critical of their neighbors, much more so than people who are at work. People who are at work don't notice neighbors parking in their driveway during the day, or the neighbors' workmen parking illegally, loud music playing, a new hedge being planted, don't notice a lot of things. But when you're at home, as are many elderly or housebound people, these daily events can become irritants—and quickly.

If you're spending time at home, take a break from looking at your neighbor's house. Pretend—convince yourself, if it's possible—that you aren't really at home, because it's a workday. If you see a problem during business hours, that problem doesn't count.

Sadly, it's sometimes the case that the only way to get rid of a weird neighbor is to move yourself. Your neighbors have a lot to do with how well—or how awfully—you live. Crooks, criminals out on bail, insane people (or people who are about to become insane), mobsters, spies, international terrorists—all have to live somewhere. And some of them might just end up next door to you. If it happens, you should consider moving, because generally, the weirder the neighbor, the less likely *he* is to move.

If you do decide to move, show your house in the wintertime. Fewer houses are on the market in winter, and there's a reasonable chance that your neighbor will be inside with the window shut. Not so during the warmer months.

Under what circumstances should you declare defeat and move? Here are a couple of cases:

*I live in a fairly nice neighborhood in an area that is considered prestigious, although it's actually not that great. We have half-acre lots, which is probably why.*

*Next door to me is a very small house which was owned by a nice couple when we moved in. A couple of years ago they divorced and the house was sold. First it sat vacant for months. Then it was rented.*

*You've heard the stereotype of the welfare queen, you've heard stereotypes about "poor white trash," and you've heard people protesting those stereotypes.*

*Well, I'm here to tell you that stereotypes exist. Because the prototypes live next door to me. What we have is an enormously fat* woman with perpetually dirty hair, tattoos, and three children she is raising by primal-scream theory. I have heard these children speak intelligibly only a few times, when they were whining at me to give them vegetables from my garden. E.g., "Gimmeeeee sommmeeee . . . gimmeeee sommmee . . . "

Then there's her "significant other." Don't know if they're married; he seems to come and go. Also dirty, also tattooed, usually drunk.

I'm positive he's been in jail at least once—I recognized him from a newspaper article. When he's there he lies in the house with the TV blaring while a baby cries and he screams obscene language at her.

They conveniently leave their windows open (the ones that aren't broken), so I can hear when I'm home.

They were also raising pit bulls at one time. For a while we had another couple of lowlifes hanging over their front fence with their pit bulls, and while the dogs would go at each other through the fence, they would talk about how great pit bulls are. Same pit bulls mangled my cat (he recovered) and several other neighborhood cats, which didn't.

Last summer they moved in some other stereotypes—who parked an RV in the back yard, dug a pit (for a latrine? I don't know for sure, but I had suspicions), and chained yet another dog out there.

They lived there for at least four months, with the man staggering around drunk half the time. I never saw them do anything except hang up more laundry outside.

Now spring is on its way again and the children are running around screaming once more. I'm not good at ages, so I don't know if they're supposed to be in school—they're not, anyway. They leave toys, clothes, trash, old furniture, you name it scattered around the backyard. When the kids are bored they throw it into my yard.

What have we done about this? Not a thing. Why not? Well . . . basically I'm afraid of them. I have two dogs. What if I complained and they poisoned my dog, or something similar? I don't trust them not to do it, and we're not home during the day. I've had a bit of conversation with this woman and she is not a kind person.

So we're moving. We'd be moving anyway, because we want a bigger house and more land, but this is a big factor. How am I going to sell my house with the neighbors from hell carrying on? I don't

·

*know. I am going to put up some screening on the fence (been mean-*
*ing to do so for some time), so their backyard can't be seen, but lately*
*they've been hanging laundry on the front porch.*

*Why don't the neighbors on the other side complain? They're*
*stone-deaf and elderly, so they never go out of the house!*

## MORE STORIES

*We were really trying to get along with our neighbor. He asked*
*to borrow our box trailer to move a chair. In the spirit of cooperation,*
*we agreed, and my husband spent half a day wiring it to his Detroit*
*road hog (actually, a Buick). Then, after the light connections, etc.,*
*were hooked up, the neighbor dropped the fact that the chair he*
*wanted to move was in Miami, over a thousand miles away, and that*
*he would have the trailer for more than three weeks!*

## HARMLESS BUT NOT TRAINABLE

Much of the time you're just plain stuck with your neighbors. Some
people are so weird, so uncivilized, so disconnected from what's normal, that it's impossible to get them to change and not worth the effort to try. You can easily recognize these houses from afar—they're
what we call "junk houses," which are instantly identifiable in well-
kept neighborhoods. The good news is that the truly weird neighbors
are a tiny percentage; the bad news is that they are unresponsive to
persuasion, kindness, threats, legal action—everything.

Could you change these people? Would you want to try? Consider:

*When my wife was growing up in Philadelphia, her family lived*
*in a rowhouse next door to neighbors they called "the kooks." Both*
*husband and wife had reputedly spent time in mental institutions,*
*and they had a profoundly retarded son. Each weekend, the three of*
*them would go to the local dump to feed the stray dogs. But of course,*
*that wasn't the worst of it. For some reason, "the kooks" had a*
*vendetta against my wife's family. They would bang on the walls late*
*at night, make crank calls, holler at their house guests, and pour*
*tacks on the front steps of the house and in front of their car tires. My*

*wife's family took them to court, but to no avail. The attacks kept com-
ing until my wife's family moved out of the area. Incidentally, "the
kooks" kept their house in such poor condition that my wife's family
had a hard time selling theirs.*

Weird, unchangeable neighbors come in a variety of flavors.
Next time you think you have a neighbor problem, just think about
Kelly, who lives in a suburb of Seattle:

*I'd like to tell you about the people I fondly call "The Trolls from
Hell" better known as my next-door neighbors. Some of it is pretty
sad, and I won't dwell much on that but rather tell you some of the
more hysterical items involved with these people. I do, though, have to
tell you about when we met them.*

*Two days after we moved into our house, even before we signed
the papers, the male troll came over to our house telling us he was
putting up a chain-link fence and would we mind if he tore down our
little picket fence that the previous owner had constructed probably
ten years earlier. He noticed my daughter and asked me how old she
was. I told him she was two and a half and he told me he had a
daughter the same age. Therefore, the next day, I went over and met
the female troll and her daughter, who was, in fact, seven days
younger than my daughter. It was at this point that I found out that
the woman was extremely abusive with her children (she's got a boy
almost two years younger). That's the sad part of this story, and I
won't go into it any further. All I'll say is that in the ten years I have
lived here, it hasn't gotten much better.*

*I must point out that our trolls next door are four feet ten and
four feet eleven and just about as wide. Mrs. Troll unfortunately has
the intelligence of a woman whose parents were most likely siblings.
Not only that, she is extremely unattractive, and Mr. Troll shaves her
face once a week. He is fifteen years older than she; he is now fifty-
eight and she is forty-three, and their children are twelve and ten.
(Can you imagine what it would be like to be fifty-eight, retired, and
have two small children? Yuck!)*

*These people are strange! They buy complete new furniture
every two years, they buy new wedding rings every five years and after
Nintendo came out, they bought three Nintendos; one for each child
and one of their own. Of course, they had to buy TV's for the kids' bed-
rooms, too. Their children go to bed with the light on and Mrs. Troll*

*turns them out before she goes to bed. They had a Chinese Pug that looks just like them and he is allowed to pee in the house (guess that's why they buy new furniture every two years?).*

Being weird by itself isn't a crime. Living next to eccentric neighbors is something that most of us can get used to. If that's all they are—eccentric. When the neighbors start sharing their eccentricities, then the real problems begin. Here's Kelly again:

*A few years ago, my husband, children and I went camping for a weekend. When we got home, I drove into the back yard and noticed something was different, but being tired out, I really couldn't tell exactly what it was. Our neighbors were standing at the fence, standing over it and when we got out of the car, they said, "What do you think of the change?" I looked over and finally figured out that our four pine trees that blocked our view of their house were gone. Now, as I said, I was very tired and all I said was, "Oh, what did you do?" Then I looked closer and discovered that the whole side of our house had obviously been damaged by fire. (I later learned that the house next door to the Trolls' had been burning garbage in the fireplace—in ninety-degree weather—and the wind had blown some sparks over to our pine trees, which were gone in an instant.) In any event, after this fire, for the rest of the summer, my neighbors would put up their lawn chairs on the side of their house and watch us coming and going in our backyard. We had some friends over for a barbecue, and the Trolls sat on their side of the fence watching us have our party!*

*Fortunately, they grew bored with that by the end of summer and we haven't had to deal with it since.*

You can't do anything about neighbors like that. (The "Trolls," as Kelly calls them, prevented their pipes from freezing in the Seattle winter by letting the outside faucet run all winter long.) Neighbors like this won't budge, not because they're stubborn, or egotistic or anything like that. They won't budge because they hold a vastly different view of the world from you and me. Their priorities, values, lifestyle are just plain different. Weird neighbors, though, have to have a place to live (like everybody else) and it's the luck of the draw if they live near you.

How did Kelly deal with her neighbors?

*Simple. I ignore them, avoid them, do anything possible to keep out of their way. Since my daughter can't stand their daughter, they don't have anything to do with each other, and therefore, I don't have anything to do with them either.*

• • • • • • • • • • • • • • • • • • • • • • • • • • • • • • • • • • • • • • • • • • • • • • • • • • •

## LIVING WITH WEIRDNESS

Ignore it.
Or build a tall fence, or plant trees or fast-growing bushes.

• • • • • • • • • • • • • • • • • • • • • • • • • • • • • • • • • • • • • • • • • • • • • • • • • • •

# WHEN YOU'RE THE WEIRD NEIGHBOR

It could be you. Yes. Let's face it: from time to time *you* are the subject of neighborhood gossip. What goes on behind people's doors is a matter of utmost curiosity for nearly all of us.

But there's no reason to broadcast your weirdness (weird to other people; normal to you.) Get curtains. Use shades and blinds. That's your first defense.

Avoid cordless telephones. You can safely assume that many of your conversations are being listened to by somebody who has a scanner. Sound unlikely? Well, if you had a scanner you would probably hear some neighbor talking on his cordless telephone about the neighbors he'd spied on. If you do use a cordless telephone, never, absolutely never, talk about anything personal or private over that phone. The same admonition goes for baby monitors. These devices broadcast on the same frequencies as cordless telephones (46 to 50 MHz) and can easily be tapped into. Worse, baby monitors have sensitive microphones that pick up sounds rooms away. So through a baby monitor in your newborn's nursery, your neighbor can listen to what's going on in your bedroom. No kidding. Turn that baby monitor off when you don't need it.

Don't shout. Keep your voice down. Argue with your spouse over the Internet if you want to, but just don't yell so loudly that your neighbors learn every facet of your husband's laziness or wife's infidelity.

One neighbor found out how dangerous it can be to complain to another neighbor, especially when the apartment's walls and floor

•

are thinner than desirable. "A woman upstairs flooded my place with her washing machine and we had a big row about it. But she got her own back on me when she left by sending me a postcard from Greece, having a go at me for making so much noise in bed. It did make me feel a bit odd knowing that she was listening."

A couple in Newcastle, England, regularly woke their downstairs neighbors with the sounds of lovemaking. Said their eighty-one-year-old downstairs neighbor, "It's dreadful. I can hear them having sex for at least thirty minutes. It's worst on Saturday nights when they've had a drink." Said the woman member of the couple, "The complaints don't mean we'll stop." Some people just don't care if their neighbors are privy to their private lives.

It's best to let your neighbors hear only silence from your apartment or house and wonder how you can have such bliss in your home.

*11*

# Defenses (Fences, Antinoise Machines, Soundproofing, Blackout Curtains, and Other Devices)

The average person wants to be liked and get along with his neighbors, so there's no reason not to try talking with your problem neighbor. The first approach should be casually diplomatic. "Say, those are some stereo speakers you have there!" Try to go into the situation with a sense of compromise. Maybe you can negotiate quiet hours after eight or nine in the evening.

## A NICE TALK

A lot of people think their neighbors are mind readers. In one Washington, D.C., apartment building, a downstairs neighbor, irked by the woman upstairs playing the news too loudly at 6 A.M., took to stealing her newspaper in retaliation. Totally unaware of the radio problem, the woman came to regard the man downstairs as some sort of despicable cheapskate who wouldn't even buy his own newspaper. He hated her all the more for not realizing the missing newspaper was a message to decrease the radio volume. In the end, another resident in the small building intervened. The morning radio volume came down, and the newspaper was delivered to the rightful subscriber.

The lesson here is to talk it out. Don't assume your neighbor will realize why you're dumping your garbage in his yard. He'll think you're a weirdo and not realize his dog just tore through your trash, scattering it all over your yard.

It's best to take your conflict to a mediator as quickly as you can. You can choose a professional mediator, or perhaps a willing—that's brave—neighbor. The longer a conflict persists, the more one neighbor may be out for blood. Most of us aren't very good at achieving compromise and understanding other people's needs. But we are good at initiating lawsuits, screaming, tattling, and complaining to the authorities. We use the term "principle of the thing" to mean that we just won't compromise. Mediators are good at helping people who otherwise would only speak to each other in court.

Surprisingly, people involved in neighbor conflicts tend to have one of two different reactions: they shrink from talking with their neighbors at all, or they forcefully confront them.

Judges in small claims courts in many states can only award money. You'll need to go to a higher court if you want action like having a fence removed or making a band stop playing. If you're going to do battle in court, you'll have to spend all your free time gathering evidence. It won't be much fun, but it will keep you busy. Lawsuits are like that.

Complaining to the city or municipal government is always worth trying before filing suit. Complaining doesn't cost money; you can remain anonymous (maybe); there is bound to be some law that the neighbor is violating. Call your city council member's office or examine the city regulation books in your library—you'll find the law that your neighbor is violating. Alternatively, call various agencies; your taxes support those agencies. When you report a violation that involves a fine, you'll probably get a prompt response: cities *like* to issue tickets.

If you're going to tattle on a neighbor and want to remain

anonymous, then it's important not to have complained to that neighbor beforehand. The neighbor will almost certainly know who ratted. While I advocate talking with neighbors about problems as a first step in most cases, I realize there are some people who seem oblivious to reasoned argument. If your neighbor is one of these types, then by all means forget talking and go right to the city for justice. If your neighbor does find out who did the telling, then what may happen is that the neighbor will regard the incident as a personal vendetta on your part, and simply dig in for a long fight. Choose your tactics carefully.

But talking is still the best solution—and the best means of preventing neighbor wars. In King County, Washington, during one summer month there were over two hundred neighbor complaints to the police. In the majority of instances, the complaining party did not even know their neighbor's name. It is indeed odd that people would rather talk to a police officer than their neighbor. Says one Washington state cop, "People don't want to talk to their neighbors; they often don't even know who they are. Instead of talking to each other, they talk to an armed police officer. That's a drastic change. People used to want to be a part of their neighborhood."

It's true that your neighbor could be odd, or even dangerous, and that talking with him might be risky. But usually not. Better still, why wait until you have a problem with your neighbor before introducing yourself? By making a point of knowing who your neighbors are, and knowing them as well as you can, you will be far less likely to need to call the police.

## CALLING THE POLICE

It's always better that you don't. The police treat neighbor disputes as a low priority. They will usually respond, but slowly (although maybe not at all in some big cities). When the police stop by, don't expect them to arrest anybody. On the contrary, the police are interested in helping defuse the dispute, especially by cooling tempers in the short run. That may be the most important role they can play.

Some conflicts get so out of control that there just doesn't seem to be anything that anybody can do to stop it. The hatred is so intense that there is nothing anybody can do to repair these bent feelings.

Look at what happened to the Weatherlys and the Williamses,

whom I talked about in the chapter on Property Wars, two very nice couples, according to their neighbors. The Weatherlys and Williamses lived in a well-kept, middle-class suburb of St. Petersburg, Florida.

One day, Mr. Weatherly was pulling out of his driveway and was hit by another car. He claimed that the accident, which was minor, occurred because he couldn't see over the Williamses' hedge. The Williamses agreed to have the hedge trimmed, but then the Weatherlys, for spite, called the police to have the trimming stopped.

Then Al Weatherly dressed up in women's clothing to participate in a charity show along with other men from his office. He went over to the Williamses' house (at this time, they were still friends— who knows why) to have his picture taken. But the Williamses were angry about the hedge incident and, according to Weatherly, "Next thing we know, the picture went all over the neighborhood and it was 'Look Flower is a transvestite.'"

Minor skirmishes ensued: trash dumped in yards; tulips trampled; pizza delivery at midnight—with fourteen pizzas in hand, all anchovy. Anonymous complaints caused the Williamses to be issued citations for "over height hedges."

Both sides wanted allies, so they called the police. Here are some samples from the police blotter. The point of retelling the story here, is to give a view of this neighbor dispute from the police's perspective:

*3/14/90 Reference neighborhood dispute that began approximately one year ago. Mrs. Williams stated that on several occasions he (Al Weatherly) has become verbally abusive. He was screaming obscenities and frightening her. Mrs. Esther Weatherly said he yelled at Williams and her husband because they feed birds fish, who then drop the fish into his pool. He also stated the Williamses awakened at (5 A.M.) and begin spying on him.*

*8/15/90 Weatherly advised that for the past few months, he has had a problem with his next-door neighbor. Stated neighbor will talk about him to various other neighbors. They watch him while he is in the yard working. Stated they have installed outside lights that shine in the couple's window.*

*8/19/90 Al Weatherly called reference ongoing problems with several neighbors. Someone had placed five beer and soda cans at the end of his driveway.*

*11/26/90 Complainant (Liza Williams) requested I go by her neighbor's house and advise him to quit harassing her. Apparently argument is over the property line.*

*12/20/90 Liza Williams advised that her neighbor, Al Weatherly, was scaring her. . . . He often curses at her and accuses her of doing things to his property. He (Weatherly) came out of his residence and started yelling and cursing. He yelled, "I'm tired of that bitch harassing me." I advised him he was disrupting the neighborhood. He invited me inside and I also spoke to his wife. Mr. Weatherly became even more irate and he took off his eyeglasses and threw them across the room.*

*8/4/91 Liza Williams called about a strange neighbor. Advised the subject (Al Weatherly) is threatening in nature and his actions have frightened her even more. Advised subject stared her down, followed her in his van.*

*9/30/91 (Esther) Weatherly said neighbors took down two sections of plastic fence between their property lines.*

*10/7/91 Complainant Louis Williams said someone destroyed his plants and threw them against his kitchen window.*

*10/8/91 Al Weatherly stated he is having ongoing problems with neighbor Liza Williams. Said he observed her running from the bushes by his house.*

*Checked area and found nothing wrong.*

One police officer had this to say about calling the cops for neighbor problems:

*For the last fifteen years, I've been a police officer in a large suburb of Chicago. During that time, I and the other officers of my force (and every other) have spent entirely too much of our time on people who are intent on winning the neighbor war.*

*So, I have some requests. In today's world, each of us must accept a certain amount of irritation from neighbors and strangers. Example: If your neighbor is playing his radio too loud to suit you on a Sunday afternoon while he washes his car, that irritation will probably end soon whether you call the police or not.*

*Relax. Some things you do irritate others, too.*

*Second, please let them know that the quickest way to resolve a situation is to speak to the person who is bothering them. Too many people call the police to address problems that have no public safety or law enforcement aspect whatever.*

•

*We're not "too busy" to respond to neighbor disputes, but rather that police intervention is not an appropriate solution to most neighbor problems.*

*For example, if you have some kind of minor disagreement with a neighbor, does sending a uniformed guy carrying a gun over to speak to him increase or decrease the chance of working out a satisfactory way of both of you living in relative peace? Most of the time this kind of thing will raise the level of tension and introduce a new roadblock to overcome if the situation is ultimately to be resolved.*

One of the most difficult situations to deal with—and fortunately one of the rarest—is when your neighbor is your landlord, and he's also a problem. What's nearly as bad is if your problem neighbor is the landlord's lover. Here's how one apartment dweller dealt with such a situation:

*Last year I moved into a four-unit small apartment building that was being pseudomanaged by one of the tenants, Nina. The landlord had given her some small responsibilities in exchange for a modest rent reduction. So she had developed a relationship of trust with the landlord and was very protective and territorial about her relationship with him.*

*When I moved in I saw that the backyard was paved over and quite ugly. I went to Nina and the landlord and offered to break up the pavement and lay down sod, grass seed, and plant flowers. I was willing to pay for half of the materials and donate all the labor. The landlord agreed to my plan and allowed a small budget for the project. Nina was at first neutral to mildly helpful but, as the project neared completion more quickly than she had thought, she became more aloof and distant. It pissed her off that someone else was doing something that would please the landlord and thus threaten the choke hold she had on the landlord's trust.*

*Just as the project was finishing up Nina purposely thwarted my plans to finish the project by swaying the landlord into doing what she wanted. Needless to say, I was furious after all the work I had done. The problem was compounded by the fact that the landlord had many years of experience with Nina and only a few scant weeks with me. This meant that even if I went to the landlord and explained the situation that it just wasn't in his best interest to believe me. He was understandably more interested in maintaining his long-term relationship with Nina.*

*I kept my calm and was diplomatic and even solicitous of Nina's friendship, but she had suddenly turned cold. She then waged a small campaign against me to try and drive me out, or at least make life miserable for me. I caught her in numerous small lies. It almost seemed as if she needed to have an adversarial relationship with the people that lived around her because she didn't know how to be their friend.*

*I decided to fight back. I am not particularly proud of what I did, but it still gives me a shameful sense of satisfaction to think back on what I did to poor Nina.*

*I knew that Nina worked at a mid-size computer software company in the area. I also knew that Nina was quite dishonest and had stolen a computer terminal from the company. I called the company security officer and reported her.*

*I waited for a while, but Nina didn't lose her job immediately. And as the situation began to deteriorate I realized that sometimes the best way to win a fight is to not fight at all. So I tendered my thirty-day notice to the landlord, who, being innocent of the feud that was going on, was quite surprised. I wasn't on speaking terms with Nina, but I sensed that her sense of "triumph" was mixed with a sense of loss at not being able to lock horns with me.*

*I wrote a parting letter detailing all of Nina's crimes against humanity, sure that it would at least make the landlord think twice before completely trusting Nina again.*

*I went out and found a new beautiful place to live that had a lot of great people and I have lived happily ever after. I was very glad that I cut my losses and ran, rather than stubbornly standing toe-to-toe with Nina in a battle that would have made me unhappy even if I had won.*

*I later found out that Nina had lost her job and moved out.*

*So I guess I did win that battle too.*

I wouldn't ever recommend this route, so I offer it here as an example of what one creatively desperate human being did.

One of my favorite reports came from this Midwesterner, who finally figured out what to do about her obnoxious neighbors.

•   •   •

•

*My reply to all of the unseemly (and seamy) things my neigh-*
*bors have done over the years was to decide, at age fifty, to teach my-*
*self how to play the trombone. Now, every evening, weather*
*permitting, I sit in my backyard patio, beverage at side, and "hoot"*
*for an hour. Amazing how many cars start up at that time of day, and*
*depart without bothering to warm up! Trouble is, after several years of*
*this, I'm actually starting to sound pretty good! (I think.)*

Creativity counts. Some solutions to your neighbor problems
involve yelling at your neighbor, calling the police, filing complaints
with the appropriate department—all regular stuff. But if you're really inventive you can get results. Here's what one architect did to
get revenge on a neighbor who caused too much trouble:

*A friend of our family's, a first family of our southern city, who*
*lives in an exclusive area of the city known for its huge houses, took ex-*
*ception to some townhouses built close by the entry of his subdivision.*
*The townhouses were well built and fit in with the neighborhood's pas-*
*tiche, but to this lawyer friend of ours, too densely developed. The ar-*
*chitect/developer of the site, also of first-family lineage, was taken to*
*court about the development and the ruling handed down was that the*
*development was indeed too dense and that he had to tear it down. Of*
*course none of this had to do with the fact that the complainant's fa-*
*ther was a former governor of the state. . . .*
*The architect, rather than tear the place down (a ridiculous*
*step) agreed to split the townhouses apart and remove parts of them,*
*at great expense.*
*This was acceptable to the court and my friend, who was happy*
*about the outcome until he awoke to see the offending townhouse sit-*
*ting right in front of his stately home on a truck. The architect, at*
*great expense, had bought the piece of property across from the*
*lawyer's house and relocated the townhouse there, a great thumb in*
*the lawyer's eye.*

## CALLS TO THE AUTHORITIES

If confrontation makes you uneasy, try an anonymous call to the authorities. (Preferably animal control, the zoning inspector, plumbing

inspector, health department, or other agency; not the police, who have better things to do with your tax dollars.)

If your neighbor's violation is against the law—barking dogs, rodent-attracting rubbish, or overgrown shrubs—perhaps a code enforcement officer will do your work for you. The officials should appreciate the tip, since they usually don't have the staff to cruise around looking for violations. So don't wait for the officials to notice the problem; you've heard of the squeaky wheel, right?

Calls to the authorities can sometimes be the prelude to a successful lawsuit, especially if the neighbor was cited. In Amherst, Massachusetts, one dog owner spent eleven thousand dollars defending herself in court because of her barking dog. She lost.

Be prepared to face defeat if you call on the authorities. Your neighbors may have some powerful and persuasive friends. Neighbors of Christine and Joel Forde thought they had an easy case. The Fordes had commissioned Los Angeles area artist Nancy Civak to construct a sculpture for their backyard, which overlooks the ocean. The sculpture was thirty old water heaters and two house trailers, entwined in the branches of their backyard pine tree. The neighbors complained it was an eyesore. The Fordes contended it was art. Weighing in the Fordes' corner: the chief curator for exhibits at the Hirshhorn Museum and Sculpture Gardens of the Smithsonian Institution; the director of education and acting head of the curatorial department of the Newport Harbor Art Museum; and the director of the Laguna Art Museum.

The Laguna Beach Design Review Board decided the work could be constructed as long as the Fordes made sure their hedges and trees hid the piece from neighbors. Still, reporting a violation to the authorities is worth a try.

Sometimes calling the authorities can backfire. One woman called the animal control department when her neighbors' dog indelicately pooped on the property line. The trouble is, the officers told the dog's owner who made the complaint. That didn't help relations between the neighbors, and so the dog owner put up a fence. But the problem wasn't really solved because the dog still roamed, played in traffic, and marked neighborhood yards with his calling card.

•  •  •

•

## THE LETTER

Alternatively, you might try writing a letter to your problem neighbor if you're not ready to call in the law. A letter is always a follow-up to a visit, though.

Simply writing an angry letter is the coward's way out. A formal complaint will just anger your neighbor and make him disinclined to deal with you.

After you've talked and you've had no relief from your problem, then try that great American tradition the letter. If the neighbor's behavior is in violation of local law, cite the law chapter and verse, and enclose a copy of the statute. Send a copy to your lawyer. Sometimes people will respond to something in writing when they don't take notice of your verbal request. A letter means you are serious. If you're willing to follow through, threaten a lawsuit.

But maybe your neighbor is someone you don't want to offend. Your minister. Your boss. Someone with the power to take away your building permit. You might want to send an anonymous letter perhaps with a photo illustration. If your neighbor's roaming dog is making you miserable, get a snapshot of the pooch doing his business on someone's lawn. Your neighbor could be embarrassed into action. But face it, anonymous letters are cowardly in most cases. Get some backing.

## SAFETY IN GROUPS

Better yet, get some support. You're less likely to be viewed as an irritable crank if you have twenty or thirty neighbors backing you in the complaint. Maybe your homeowners association can lend a hand, or a petition drive in your neighborhood may help. (Alternatively, if none of your neighbors join you in your complaint, you might have to consider that you are an irritable crank.)

When neighbors of Mitzie and Jennings Burger in Little Rock, Arkansas, grew tired of their annual Christmas display, they gathered forces to oppose it. The Burgers' display of 1.5 billion lights attracted an estimated 20,000 visitors, who drove through the neighborhood to view the Christmas spectacle. The neighbors, tired of the traffic and crowd problems during the busy holiday season, went to court to stop the lighting, and fifty of them testified against the display. The judge took the compromise solution, limiting the days the display could be on and reminding everyone to remember the reason they celebrated Christmas.

Sometimes the power of numbers can work even without the power of the court behind you. When Bob Ugent painted his Costa Mesa, California, home lime green and orange with startling decorative tick-tack-toe patterns and other unconventional designs, his neighbors were shocked. Then angry. They banded together and pressured Ugent to repaint his home. He chose gray. His actions hadn't been illegal, and while he had every right to paint his house the way he wanted, Ugent listed to the voice of his neighbors.

One Baltimore, Maryland, homeowner liked to feed squirrels. Several of his neighbors had small children and were concerned that one of the children might get bitten by a squirrel. So they asked, and this neighbor stopped.

Besides, talking to your neighbors might save some embarrassment. Had one woman talked first to her neighbors before calling the authorities, some neighbors in New England might be on better terms:

*On Halloween a woman came by with her child and introduced herself as the neighbor three houses down from us. We all own two acres, so there is a distance between us. She was complaining about a helicopter that used to fly too low over the neighborhood. Her husband, a weekend pilot, got their camera with a zoom lens and took a picture of the tail of the helicopter for the call letters. When they had it developed they called the FAA to report the pilot. I listened to her story, then told her that pilot was my husband. He is a corporate pilot who flies helicopters and jets, and during that summer he went to Hampton, New Hampshire, a lot and flew around the neighborhood. A lot of other neighbors would go out and wave to him! I was sorry she felt that she had to report to the FAA.*

*She left right after I told her it was my husband, that he has been flying for twenty-five years, and that he would never take chances by flying too low. He was low but within regulations.*

. . .

.

# TO SUE OR NOT TO SUE

Lawsuits. That's what America is about. The right to sue. The privilege to sue. The joy of suits. But it isn't always worth it and it isn't always possible. In very general terms, you probably aren't going to win against a nuisance neighbor if you knew about that neighbor before you moved onto the block, and if other neighbors tolerate the so-called nuisance, and if the nuisance doesn't break any laws. For example, if your neighbors are social butterflies, always holding parties, and if the slamming of car doors as guests come and go bothers you and you alone, well, then—you're probably out of luck.

Filing a civil suit is your last resort and a drawn-out, expensive one too. The suit may drag on for years, and destroy you emotionally and financially. Judges hate these suits too, so you might not get a sympathetic hearing. Your claim of damage from a neighbor's tree will pale in comparison to an asbestos-damage case. Many judges refer neighbor-versus-neighbor lawsuits to mediators, so you might as well try that first. (The vast majority of cases handled by mediators are referred by the courts.) At least a mediated solution is one you and your neighbor draw up while the court's solution is one the judge dreams up.

The American Bar Association distributes a directory of 420 not-for-profit programs and hundreds of private practitioners who will mediate disputes for a fee. The ABA section of dispute resolution operates a resource center that offers basic advice as well as referrals to mediation services.

During mediation a professional guides you and your neighbor to a reasonable solution to the problem. People who choose mediation almost always reach an agreement—and abide by it.

While some people are going into second and third appeals and years of litigation, others are living contentedly with their mediated solution. The difference between being told what to do and deciding what to do yourself is the key here.

More than anything else, I'm an advocate of staying out of the courts. Unless the offense is so egregious (for example, your neighbor goes away for the weekend and his home whiskey still explodes, destroying your garage, and he does nothing about it) that it begs for a lawsuit, a lawsuit is probably not worth it. So when your neighbor's tree falls on your house, when his kid beats up yours, when his dog impregnates yours, consider your options: relaxing evenings spent with family and friends or tense evenings spent alone hunched over legal briefs. Try these alternatives:

- Mediation: Face-to-face, across-the-table communication facilitated by a neutral person.
- Arbitration: A hearing at which disputants may offer evidence and witnesses. The disputants agree to abide by the decision reached by a neutral person.
- Conciliation: A process of independent communication between the disputants and a neutral person.

## TO COURT

When all else fails, consider the courts. That is, if you have lots of extra time, money, and emotional currency. And if you never want to have a cordial relationship with your neighbor again. And remember, after the case is settled, you still have to live near your neighbor—win or lose!

Still, some intractable neighbors invite lawsuits. "So sue me," they taunt. So do. Research your neighbor's pesky habit; maybe it's illegal. (If it's illegal enough—relentless, deafening noise, for instance—the police or some government agency will handle the problem for you). Once you have a good strategy, you're ready to go to court.

The cheapest place to start is in small claims court. You won't need a lawyer there, but claims are limited in most states to one or two thousand dollars. If a few thousand doesn't faze your neighbor, have some neighbors join in the suit for equal amounts. That should rouse him from his unneighborly attitude. You won't need an attorney for a small claims court suit; your only costs will be a small filing fee and the expenses for the research and copying of documents.

You need to be well organized when you go to court so that you appear more reasonable and better prepared than your neighbor. Take along photos that support your case, copies of letters, a neighbor or expert to testify on your behalf, and any other documentation that supports your claim.

•   •   •

•

## FACE TO FACE BEATS LAWYER TO LAWYER

Courts are also well suited to creating winners and losers, which is fine if the parties don't ever plan to talk again. But breeding winners and losers is not the best solution among neighbors, who, in some way or another, have to live with each other.

Frequently neighbor fights just get out of hand. With egos in charge, they escalate until nobody is in control any more.

Take the feud between the Talcotts and the Joneses, for example. It started innocently enough, when Talcott complained to Jones that the landscaper's tractor was too noisy to be operating at 7 A.M. In fairness, this is a common neighbor complaint—contractors just don't have the same concern for neighbors that most neighbors do, or should have. Jones said, fine, and that should have been that. Then, Talcott called the fire department to complain about illegal burning on the Joneses' property. Talcott said that the fire department was already in the neighborhood and that all he did was direct them to the location of the fire. Soon after that, Jones's landscaper told Mr. Jones that Talcott had threatened him. Talcott wrote Jones a letter in which he said, "It is unfortunate we have to live with a person like you on our street. This has, until now, been a nice street to live on, with nice, reasonable neighbors. You are obviously a disturbed person and I want no dealings with you whatsoever."

This was not a constructive letter. Don't mimic it.

To anybody watching this conflict from a distance, it was pretty clear that reconciliation between these neighbors would take heroic efforts. Alas, neither Jones nor Talcott was a hero. Periodic shouting ensued.

Talcott came over to Jones's house, ostensibly to apologize, but the incident erupted in shouting. Jones called 911. From that moment on, the two neighbors communicated only through attorneys.

The conflict spread throughout the neighborhood. Some time later, Talcott erected a satellite dish in his backyard. A neighbor or two complained to the building department—it may or may not have been Jones who complained. Immediately after that, Talcott filed an antiharassment suit against Jones and three other neighbors. When this case got to court, the neighbors said that they hardly knew the Talcotts; one neighbor said that he had never met the Talcotts and had only spoken to the Joneses twice in two years. This neighbor lived across the street from both.

During this time the building department had paid Jones numerous visits because of complaints, so Jones filed an antiharassment suit against Talcott.

After some time, the Joneses moved away. And so did the Talcotts. Said Talcott: "I didn't intend to meet our neighbors. But if I had known what kind of people they were, we never would have moved here." To fund this battle, Talcott sold his stocks and deferred payment on his life insurance.

• • • • • • • • • • • • • • • • • • • • • • • • • • • • • • • • • • • • • • • • • • • • • • • • • •

## WHAT TO DO WHEN YOUR NEIGHBOR SUES

The first thing you should do when your neighbor threatens to sue you (and I'm speaking here as a neighbor, not a lawyer) is to call that neighbor on the phone. Say, "I'm really sorry that we have a bad dispute between us. I'd like to do something to help resolve it. Would you like to come over for coffee so we can talk about making amends?"

If your neighbor says, "No," you're no worse off than before you called. If your neighbor says, "Yes," then anything is possible. Just look at Israel and the PLO.

• • • • • • • • • • • • • • • • • • • • • • • • • • • • • • • • • • • • • • • • • • • • • • • • • •

The Stanislaus County Board of Supervisors had a great idea. Stanislaus County is a vibrant farming region in California. It's a place where there's crop dusting, manure aromas, flies, animal and machinery noises—the regular cacophony that accompanies farming. Stanislaus County is in the San Joaquin Valley, which is composed of eight counties and produces 61 percent of California's farmed goods. Developers make a bundle from selling land to potential home builders, and home builders are willing to pay a bundle. While farming is profitable, developing land is even more profitable. Farming peaches, for example, yields $3,293 per acre; selling the land to developers yields $30,000.

People from the city like rural farming communities. Until they move there and discover the smells and the noises that don't seem to bother farmers. Some new residents of the San Joaquin Valley have objected to spraying, and have insisted that spraying schedules be changed so that their cars don't get dusted. Other residents have objected to early-morning spraying—too loud, they said.

•

Lately, there have been a lot more lawsuits than crops growing in the Valley.

So what's the good idea? It's right-to-farm legislation, laws designed to let people know exactly where they are moving. One bill requires real estate agents to notify prospective buyers in writing what the county is like. Another prevents land from being split into blocks of less than sixty acres. Still another proposed law prohibits development of irrigated agricultural land.

All of these proposals can be thought of as good-neighbor policies. They are, indirectly, designed to prevent neighbor-versus-neighbor conflicts. Many people don't consider what kind of neighborhood they're moving into and decide that when they arrive they don't like their new neighborhood. So they set out to change it. The only problem—and it's a big problem—is that the longtime residents *do* like the neighborhood and that's why they live there.

I've always believed that when choosing a house, it's not just the house that matters but your neighbors, too. Meet your potential neighbors before you buy. You may discover that one neighbor is a rock and roll drummer, another is an ex-felon who has his buddies over for late-night poker games, another has a woodworking shop in the basement, another rents rooms, legally, as a bed and breakfast, another has air conditioning condensers that are very, very loud.

Neither real estate agents nor home sellers are required to tell you about the pesky neighbors next door. And they won't.

Also check zoning and other regulations before you buy. What you can and can't do will have significant bearing on the relationship between you and your future neighbors. For example, subdivisions that don't allow fences (because they're "ugly") often have dog problems. Without fences, dogs roam wherever they want.

Another tip: Make sure you see the house at various time of the day and evening before you buy. If it's quietest at 10 A.M. that's because the guy who throws all-night parties every evening sleeps late. Drive by the house at midnight once or twice, and especially over a weekend.

Almost nobody considers who the neighbors are going to be when they examine property. But everybody should. The best way to deal with unruly neighbors is not to move in next to them.

Anticipating problems and then preventing them is a grand idea, assuming, of course, that these preventative measures are legal and ethical. Not getting into fights is the best way to resolve fights.

If all else fails, remember: Good fences make good neighbors. (Apologies to Robert Frost.)

## SWEET, PETTY REVENGE

In Paris, New Jersey, a woman spent years tending to her spite garden, designed to get revenge on her neighbors.

Her neighbor had filed a complaint with the city housing agency about a small playhouse she'd made for her child. Although the house was permitted to stand, the woman was angry and felt her neighbor was always falsely accusing her. In revenge the woman hung underwear on a clothesline in the backyard, never taking it down and always adding to it, so that she had an outlandish collection of extra-large and colorful underwear. It was a revenge line, a harmless tactic, and the woman can pour all her frustration into it in creative ways.

## ALTERNATIVE WAYS TO PEACE

Sometimes it pays to ignore your neighbor and simply erect whatever defenses you can envision—or afford. There are times when yelling, building fences, hauling your neighbor into court, or buying a bigger dog just aren't effective. Your neighbor might be a lot bigger than you, for example. Or your neighbor might be just too nice to complain to.

Whatever you decide, be sure to keep your sense of proportion during the dispute or you could be in worse trouble than when you started. George Moser in suburban Chicago could have used this lesson. After two years of waiting for the courts to settle a boundary dispute he had with his neighbors, he took action. One day he brought in a bulldozer to tear up a section of his neighbor's drive that had been built on his lot. Although his neighbors, Kenneth and Carla Jackson, shouted at the bulldozer operator to stop, Moser had him continue his work. The Jacksons sued Moser for $1 million. The case is still pending.

●   ●   ●

●

## Special Noise Strategies

No doubt the number one neighbor complaint is about noise. Clip-clopping high heels on tile. Booming music. Noise is all around us, from the radio blasting in our cars to the chatter around the dinner table. But these are noises we choose. What about the banging of a neighbor's basketball at 8 o'clock on a Sunday morning? Another person's enjoyment is your nuisance, and you can't always remedy the situation.

Machines to measure decibels are available for gathering evidence. Check your local electronics store and get to work.

Antinoise headsets, also called automatic noise reduction headsets (ANR), have just arrived in the consumer marketplace. For years they were available only in specialty markets—for pilots, for instance. (When I fly my plane I wear a pair of ANRs; they block out most of the Cessna engine's noise.) Now, for about one hundred dollars, you can buy a pair guaranteed to make the neighbor's drumming, or leaf blowing, or yelling virtually vanish. ANRs work by creating antinoise, a sound wave that's opposite in amplitude and wavelength to what's entering your ears. The downside of ANRs is that they're available only as headsets. But the quiet is bliss.

You can also cocoon yourself in a more pleasurable noise. Try tapes of nature sounds: bird songs, waterfalls, streams, ocean, rain, and other sounds. Many trendy high tech stores carry white noise machines for about one hundred dollars. White noise is a steady, soothing hiss that filters out high-frequency sounds. Some of them let you choose from several soothing sounds like rain, waterfalls, and the ocean.

Earplugs are surprisingly effective, and if you can get used to sleeping with them in your ears, you're set. The foam kind are the best, and you can get them at most drugstores. Or go a step up and get some earplugs many rock musicians use. They're about ten times as expensive, but it's a small price to pay for a little peace.

Soundproofing is another alternative. If you can swing a more elaborate solution, you may get more relief. You need to stop the offending sound as close to the source as possible. So you want to keep your neighbor's noises in your neighbor's apartment and the garbage truck noises outside.

A good contractor can help you soundproof a room. Often they'll build a room within a room, which unfortunately, reduces the room's overall size. But the tradeoff may be worth it to you. The trick is to leave a few centimeters of space between the walls, space that will create a sound barrier.

To keep the din of traffic to a minimum, try adding storm windows and sound-absorbing drapes. The more layers, the more sound protection.

There are special acoustical linings for drapes. Let the drapes or shades extend beyond the window edges.

Some people even upholster the walls to help cut down on noise. Loosely woven fabric goes over a cotton batting. The top layer is tacked to wood furring strips. Thick, tightly woven fabrics work best.

Wood, brick, stone, plaster, shutters, and other hard surfaces allow sound to bounce all over. Carpets and window coverings will help contain the sound, as will the more expensive options of unholstering walls, building buffer walls, or painting walls and ceiling with a textured paint filled with tiny particles that trap sound.

Try adding wood paneling and leave some dead air space between the paneling and the wall. Better yet, try adding some insulation between the paneling and wall.

## SORRY SIGHTS

A fence can do many things: keep your pets in the yard, keep the neighbor kids out, or provide a barrier between roaming dogs and your kids. A fence also simply offers privacy from prying neighbors or just hides their "vintage" car collection.

Wood fences, very popular for maintaining privacy, are expensive and becoming more so. Plastic fences and plastic-coated wire fences are becoming more popular. More costly than wood, plastic tends to have a longer life span. It's colorfast, so you don't have to paint it every few years. Some vinyl fences are stronger than wood.

Also try planting some fast-growing plants. Vines like morning glory will soon obliterate every hint of the nuisance. Ivy is an even better cover, since it doesn't need to be replanted every year.

Alternatively, place a folding screen in front of your window. It lets light in, allows you to look out if you really want to, yet keeps people on the street from peering in. Shades that raise from bottom to top are also useful for bringing privacy back to your life.

•

Blackout shades work wonders for protection from your neighbor's security lights and holiday display. If you use them in conjunction with some noise abatement tools, you'll think you're the only person left on earth.

• • • • • • • • • • • • • • • • • • • • • • • • • • • • • • • • • • • • • • • • • • • • • • • •

### RESOURCES

The catalog from Walpole Woodworkers features fencing materials and do-it-yourself kits (Walpole Woodworkers, 767 East St., Walpole, Mass. 02081. Phone: 800-343-6948).

TAB / McGraw-Hill has published a third edition of *Fences, Decks and Other Backyard Projects,* by Dan Ramsey (TAB Books, $24.95 hardcover, $14.95 paper).

For your legal bookshelf:

*Neighbor Law: Fences, Trees, Boundaries & Noise,* by Cora Jordan (Nolo Press, $14.95).

*Neighbor Vs. Neighbor: Legal Rights of Neighbors in Dispute* (Sphinx Publishing, $ 12.95).

*The Law of Trees,* privately published by Sid D. Merulla. (Send $20 to Mr. Merulla at 772 South Front Street, Columbus, Ohio 43206.) Merulla, an Ohio lawyer, is former assistant attorney general with the Ohio Department of Agriculture.

• • • • • • • • • • • • • • • • • • • • • • • • • • • • • • • • • • • • • • • • • • • • • • • •

## WHEN YOU'RE THE PROBLEM

The adage "it is better to give than receive" also applies to neighbor relations. Right? Much better to be the *giver* of loud music than the *receiver* of noise. But we rarely consider ourselves to be nuisances—it's always the other guy who's a menace to civilization.

From time to time neighbors approach us with requests, some reasonable, some absolutely insane. Your first obligation as a good neighbor is to listen to your neighbor as he describes the problem. You can bet that whatever the problem is, it's been festering in your neighbor's mind for quite a while. By the time he speaks to you about it, he has had to decide between talking with you gently about the problem and screaming at you. In all likelihood, gentle talking wins, by a slight margin. Do your neighbor a favor and pay attention. Look at him. Nod your head (you can always shake it later). Don't feign listening, because your neighbor may actually have something important to say.

But what do you say? You don't have to agree to change your ways initially. But the first words from your mouth should be words of apology; something along the lines of, "I'm sorry, I didn't know that our cat was using your vegetable garden as a litter box. I'm really sorry."

You've accomplished two important goals initially: first you have convinced your neighbor that what he has to say is important to you, just as it is important to him; second, you have humbled yourself by apologizing. Nobody likes to beat up on a humbled man or woman.

Already the situation is better, but you still haven't resolved the conflict. Before agreeing or disagreeing with your neighbor, there's one more step you can take to help relax the situation: Subtly paint your neighbor as a minority. Say, "Oh, I'm sorry. Everybody thinks that Socks is such a cute cat, and I guess nobody else has complained about him in their garden. Gee, all the children in the neighborhood just love him." Nobody likes to be considered an outcast, or worse, a jerk. Although this kind of remark probably won't change your neighbor's point of view about your cat, it may temper his anger. Now your neighbor not only has to consider your feelings but has to take into account the opinions of other people in the neighborhood. The stage is set, and now both sides can discuss the issue reasonably.

Of course, from this point on you and your neighbor have to deal with the substance of the problem, which in this case is your cat pooping in your neighbor's garden. *If you can,* and assuming you want to, make every attempt to correct the problem. Let your neighbor know at each step what you're doing. Invite your neighbor to offer possible solutions, too. If changing your cat's behavior is going to take some time, then let your neighbor know that, as well.

Sometimes it's not the problem per se that's causing trouble but the fact that you aren't aware that something's the matter. Your neighbor may think that you are taking advantage of him, that you're not a considerate neighbor—and these thoughts may be just as important to him as what your cat actually does. The more heroic your efforts appear when trying to solve the problem, the more you have done to defuse any potential conflict.

Next step, home-baked cookies. Presenting your neighbor with a plate of home-baked cookies makes it next to impossible for him to get angry at you. After all, you've demonstrated that you are sincerely nice, or something like that. If cookies aren't appropriate, a bottle of wine works, too; or just invite your neighbors over for dinner or dessert.

Money can work wonders, too. Money can also insult your neighbor, so use its powers wisely.

# 12

# How to Be a Good Neighbor

### How to Be a Perfect Neighbor

Welcome each new neighbor with a plate of cookies.

Ban all leaf blowers from your property.

Train your dog not to bark, and always leash your dog.

Give your teenagers headphones for their stereos and enforce their use.

Don't snoop.

Smile each time you see your neighbor.

Offer to take care of your neighbor's newspapers and mail while he's away.

Don't put up a basketball hoop in your front yard, or beneath your neighbor's bedroom or family room.

Talk with your neighbors before you start any construction projects.

Talk with your neighbors regularly. Know their names and use their names.

Give them a copy of this book.

........................................................

## Winning Your Neighbors Over

The most important step in winning the neighbor wars is to avoid conflicts altogether. If your neighbors are crazy about you, they'll probably do whatever they can to fix what's bothering you. Californian Judy Pepper makes it tough for her neighbors to hate her. Here's one way to win hearts:

*We have made it a point to make something special at holidays, like cookies, and let the kids deliver it to our neighbors. We also share from our fruit trees. When we first moved into the neighborhood, our neighbors seemed a little reclusive and also concerned about kids living next door. (Both of our immediate neighbors are in their late sixties and early seventies.) Now they enjoy talking with our daughters. We have lived in our current house for three years and our daughters are five and seven.*

Nancy Bloom, a Colorado food writer and cookbook author, finds a similar tack works for her. She keeps her neighbors happy with a steady supply of goodies when she's testing new dessert recipes.

Being a good neighbor is probably the best strategy for having good neighbors, as these people have discovered.

## What Do You Do If Your Neighbors Are *Too* Nice?

Is there such a thing? Well, yes—and it happens this way. Your neighbor volunteers to help you with a project, such as removing a tree, fixing a roof, or repairing a car. Your neighbor might be helpful, but helpful isn't helpful if your neighbor isn't competent. Here's an example:

*We had a row of lombardy poplars at the back of our property and our neighbor had a similar stand at the back of his property a few years earlier but had taken them down because the roots were working their way into his swimming pool. When ours started to die, I went out and removed some branches from one of them to see how difficult it might be to take them down myself. They were at least twenty-five to thirty feet tall. When my neighbor saw me in the yard and saw what I was doing (we were talking at this point), he came out to investigate. When he discovered that I was figuring how difficult it would be to take them down, he offered to help. I thanked him but said no as my son and my son-in-law to be would help. He persisted to the point that I finally gave in but said I couldn't start right away as I had some errands to run. He again persisted and said that he could get some of it done while I was running around.*

*Again I gave in but said that he was to do no more than take the lower branches off (up to about eight feet). When I returned home a few hours later, the trees were a mess. Several had had the top fifteen feet taken off, my yard was littered with branches, and my telephone and cable TV lines were down. Some trees had been cut into in such a way that there was no way I could finish the job but would have to hire professionals to finish. He sent his son over with the story that some neighbor boys were passing and offered to do the job and he let them.*

*He promised to pay for the installation of the cable and telephone lines but said nothing, through his son, about the remaining twelve trees. His son later came over on his own and explained that his father tackled the job when he was drunk and did the damage. It cost me $150 to have someone come in immediately (because of the condition of the trees) and take down the remaining trees, when I feel I could have done the job at my leisure at no cost. I took the next week to chop up the logs for firewood.*

## THE PERPETUAL COMPLAINER

The hardest neighbors to be nice to are the ones who perpetually complain. You know the type, I'm sure. They find fault with everything about you and your house. They don't like your shrubs; they think your bumper sticker is offensive; they think your toilets are too loud. And so forth.

Meet Max, a Phoenix, Arizona, neighbor who fits that bill perfectly, as I was told by his neighbor, Phil:

*I had a neighbor named Max who lived two doors to the east of my house. His complaints included my dogs' barking (they did), their pooping on his lawn (they didn't), telling one neighbor that he didn't want him running his outdoor hot tub because it made too much noise, and noticing that there was a white residue in the gutter in front of his house after some workmen from our house rinsed out some buckets after doing some drywalling.*

*Max outdid himself, though, when he complained about the barbecuing that my neighbor to the west, Rich, used to love to do. Rich got a visit from Max one weekend, explaining that he didn't like the fumes from the barbecue lighter fluid Ron was using (three houses away!) and he had bought Rich an electric charcoal lighter.*

Phil and Rich's predicaments are fairly common. A family I know who lives just a few blocks away has gotten calls from his neighbor three houses away because the family is barbecuing. This neighbor tells my friends to move their grill to the other side of their deck so that the smoke won't waft over into his house. (The same complainer had this family ticketed for putting their garbage can out on the wrong day.)

There's no perfect way to deal with a perpetual complainer. One technique is not to go along with this neighbor's demands—but rather pretend to. Just say, "Sure, we'll move our barbecue," or, "We'll train our dogs to bark quieter." Then go on with what you're doing. The complainer likes to complain and will, no matter what you do. So you might as well just continue doing what you like best.

Alternatively, be firm and oppose your neighbor's suggestions: Say, "I'm sorry that you don't like what I'm doing, but none of my other neighbors minds. I'm not breaking the law. Let me suggest some ways to make things better for you. . . ."

If there is some basis for the neighbor's complaint—barking dogs, for example—bend a little. Do what you can to reduce the causes for any real complaints, then just use smiles and nods to take care of the rest of the complaints. Having complained to you, the complainer will go on to harass another neighbor for a while.

Perpetual complainers are usually fairly docile neighbors. Complaining for them is an art, a joy almost. So they will always find fault with you. Once you recognize that this is a game, albeit a strange one, and once you understand the rules, playing the game and winning it won't be too much trouble.

## WHAT'S WORSE

Having a perpetual complainer as a neighbor isn't all that bad, especially when you consider who else is out there.

Every problem has its own unique solution. The purpose of *Outwitting the Neighbors* is not to offer a formula for dealing with each problem, but to point out that you're going to have to be creative. You'll have to investigate by examining the causes and the nature of the person who is your problem. Here's what I mean:

*One of the neighbors was a ham radio operator, and had a phenomenal setup in his part of the building. The sounds coming through the walls didn't bother me too much, but it drove me crazy when he'd find someone overseas to talk to and crank the reception all the way up because I'd then hear their conversation quite clearly . . . coming over my toaster! It must have had something to do with the way the building was wired. Anyway, repeated requests to tone it down were met with refusals until I figured out how to sabotage his reception: I'd make a slice of toast, and the interference would be such that he'd have to either quit or find someone else to talk to.*

One Californian I interviewed recommended this strategy for dealing with a troublesome neighbor. First, resume friendship with that neighbor. Make a peace offering by buying him a cordless telephone. Then get yourself a scanner and a tape recorder. . . . Well, you get the idea. Illegal to say the least, but it should accomplish what is necessary.

## WHAT'S NEXT?

This book can only prepare you for what you might encounter in that strange, ever changing universe of neighborhoods. Your reality may be worse than anything I've described in this book, because it's real for you.

But maybe not. Whatever happens there's somebody else who's suffering more than you are. And they'll continue to suffer as long as they don't make peace with their neighbors, or, failing that, don't defeat their neighbors.

Good luck.

# INDEX

•

## ABOUT THE AUTHOR

Bill Adler Jr. is the president of Adler &
Robin Books, Inc., a literary agency. He is
the author of a mountain of books including
*Outwitting Squirrels: 101 Cunning Strata-*
*gems to Reduce Dramatically the Egregious*
*Misappropriation of Seed from Your Bird-*
*feeder by Squirrels; Baby-English: A Dictio-*
*nary for Interpreting the Secret Language of*
*Infants; Outwitting Critters;* and *The Home*
*Remodeler's Combat Manual.* In his free
time, Adler is an aerobatic pilot. He lives in
Washington, D.C., with his wife, Peggy, and
two daughters, Karen and Claire. He is surrounded by wonderful neighbors. Honest.